EISENSTEIN
a Documentary Portrait

by the same author
FACTUAL TELEVISION
(Focal Press)

Chris Evans

Nov. 1980

EISENSTEIN

a Documentary Portrait

Norman Swallow

London   George Allen & Unwin Ltd
Ruskin House   Museum Street

First published 1976

© George Allen & Unwin Ltd 1976

ISBN 0 04 791034 8 (hardback)
       0 04 791035 6 (paperback)

Printed in Great Britain
in 10 point Baskerville type
by Acolortone Ltd, Ipswich, Suffolk

PREFACE

The origin of this book is a two-part television film, made for the
BBC's *Omnibus* series. It was first shown in Britain in December 1970,
and a revised version was transmitted by NET/TV (New York) in 1973.

The film had four main ingredients: the life of Eisenstein as reflected
by the places he knew, by contemporary photographs, and by quotations from his writing; selected sequences from each of his films; his
own drawings and designs, whether created for a particular film or
theatre production or merely done for personal pleasure; and the
recollections of those who knew him. That last ingredient is the core
of this book and its main justification. During the preparation and
production of the film twenty-five of Eisenstein's personal friends and
professional colleagues were interviewed at length, and many of them
on several occasions. Most of their statements were recorded, but less
than a quarter of the material was used in the completed film. Nearly
all of it is used in this book.

The book's text is otherwise based on the film's commentary, which
I wrote in collaboration with someone who worked closely with
Eisenstein in the Moscow theatre in the early 1920s, was assistant
director of *Battleship Potemkin*, and co-author and co-director of
October, Old and New, and the sadly unfinished *Que Viva Mexico!*: G. V.
Alexandrov. As he was co-producer of the BBC documentary and
played a large part in the choice of those who spoke in it (many of
whom were his personal friends) he is almost as responsible for this book
as I am myself, though it would be unfair to associate him with all the
opinions expressed in it.

In fact it contains few opinions other than those offered by
witnesses of Eisenstein's life and work. As a documentary television
producer by profession I have tried in these pages to create a documentary book. But what is a 'documentary'? I refrain from quoting
the famous definition of John Grierson, but there is a lesser known and
less romantic one by Maurice Wiggin, former television critic of *The*

Sunday Times, who once described a television documentary as a
'programme based on documents'. It is a fair summary of my method
in this book, in which the 'documents' are the words of personal
witnesses and the illustrations are chosen for their value as evidence
rather than for any intrinsic merits of their own. On those few occasions
when I have dared to express an opinion, I have done so merely to
summarize the documentary evidence.

If Eisenstein had not died at the tragically early age of fifty he
would today be an old man and would perhaps still be directing films.
It is a sad reflection, though in the circumstances hardly surprising,
that it would be quite impossible to begin work on this book today or
tomorrow, for too much of it relies on the words of those who have
died in the last few years: John Grierson, Grigori Kozintsev, Lev
Kuleshov, Mikhail Romm, Maxim Strauch. On a more personal level
Lyubov Orlova, wife of G. V. Alexandrov and star of his films in the
1930s, who was a constant source of wisdom and delight during the
making of the BBC documentary, died between the completion of this
book's text and its publication.

Many people in several countries have helped to shape the book, and
I am particularly grateful to those whose words form half of its text.
Of the many others who have generously given me the benefit of their
knowledge and wisdom I would particularly like to thank the following:
Lindsay Anderson, who read the commentary of the film and shrewdly
re-wrote many of its weakest passages; Susan Anderson, who was my
assistant on the film and who has kindly typed the manuscript of this
book; René Clair, who told me so much about Eisenstein's visit to
France; Curtis Davis, formerly of NET/TV (New York); Nikolai
Efimov and Anatoli Uglov of the Novosti Press Agency (Moscow);
Lise Hunter, who let me read in advance of publication her translation
of Ion Barna's biography of Eisenstein; Paul Humfress, editor of the
television documentary; Jay Leyda, for his advice during the preparation of the documentary; Lewis Milestone, for his personal reminiscences of Eisenstein in Hollywood; Ariadne Nicolaeff for her translations
of the Russian and for her comments on the completed text; Peter
Pagnamenta of the BBC for arranging and directing the interviews in
the USA; Marie Seton, for a most stimulating meeting; Victor
Shlovsky for his memories of Eisenstein in the USSR; and Lazar

Wechsler for all the information he gave me about Eisenstein's visit to Switzerland.

I am especially grateful to Ivor Montagu, who kindly read the text at an early stage, and made numerous helpful suggestions, and to Naum Kleiman, whose knowledge of the Eisenstein archive in Moscow made him a most valued member of the film's production team. I would also like to thank Basil Wright and the BBC for permission to use long extracts from a talk originally broadcast on the Third Programme, and Herbert Marshall and the Southern Illinois University of Carbondale for allowing me to quote an essay by Professor Marshall.

For the use of photographs and other illustrations I would like to thank G. V. Alexandrov, Ivor Montagu, Mosfilm, the National Film Archive (London), and the Novosti Press Agency (Moscow).

This book would never have been written or published had not the BBC, in 1968, given me permission to make a film about Eisenstein, and for this I am particularly grateful to Paul Fox (then Controller of BBC-1) and to Stephen Hearst (then the BBC's Head of Arts Features). Equally valuable were the decisions of NET (New York) to co-produce the film, and of the Novosti Press Agency (Moscow) to co-operate fully in its production. The BBC has also allowed me full access to the relevant correspondence and programme files, and has helped me very generously during the preparation of this book. It is also true to say that my personal ambition to make both a film and a book about Eisenstein was stimulated by my collaboration with G. V. Alexandrov on a film made by Granada Television Ltd in 1967 to mark the occasion of the 50th Anniversary of the October Revolution. For that opportunity I will always be grateful to Granada Television, and especially to Lord Bernstein and Sir Denis Forman.

Norman Swallow

CONTENTS

ILLUSTRATIONS

1

The Birth of a Director

Sergei Mikhailovich Eisenstein was born on 3 January 1898 in Riga, the seaport and capital of the Tsar's province of Latvia, an only child of parents who were to separate for ever when he was eleven. His father, Mikhail Osipovich, headed the Construction Department of the local railway company, a pedantic and much decorated man with a pronounced affection for orders, ranks, and personal flattery. He was also both an engineer and an architect, and it was in the latter capacity that his son later dismissed him as a 'maker of cakes', urging his friends to 'look at all the cream on that house's face'. Eisenstein's mother, Julia Konyetskaya, was the daughter of a largely self-made merchant of St Petersburg, a woman who regarded her husband as vulgar and in her snobbish way thought it wise that her son should grow up to become a man of culture. With this aim in mind she not only supplied him generously with books of all kinds but took him, at the age of eight, to Paris where he saw many things but remembered most of all an early film of Georges Méliès, *Four Hundred Jokes of the Devil*. In later life he looked back on his childhood and wrote these words about himself:

'Whenever I examine myself closely as a child I picture myself mostly as a David Copperfield.
  Fragile,
  skinny,
  small,
  defenceless.
  And very shy.'

For most of his adult life Latvia was no longer a part of his own country, so that when he left Riga in his teens he lost all contact with those who had been his friends at school. Yet many of them remembered the young Sergei Mikhailovich – or at least were prompted to remember him whenever they read of that 'brilliant' film director whose name was Eisenstein, and who had once been a pupil at the same school in Nikolayevsky Street. One of them, who has remained in Riga all his life and is now the city's most respected bookseller, is Erwin Mednis:

'It is seventy years since I went to school with Eisenstein, but I still remember him vividly. Physically he was slightly built, and rather frail. There was something rather feminine about his appearance, so that he often looked more like a girl than a boy. He was always very sociable, and invariably good-natured, and there can be no doubt at all that intellectually he was extremely gifted. When he came to school for the first time he could already speak two languages very well indeed: French and German. Later, but not much later, he learnt English. In those days it was his intention, if not exactly his ambition, to become a professional engineer like his father, and to pass from the school in Riga to the Institute of Civil Engineering in St Petersburg, where his precocious gift for drawing would be an enormous advantage.

'I have used that phrase "would be" very deliberately. For although his talent as a visual artist was undeniably high, and of course remained with him throughout his short life, he had a habit of placing it at the service of a mischievous sense of humour that was even higher. He spent a great deal of his time drawing caricatures of both his fellow pupils and, more dangerously, of his teachers, and he preferred to draw them during lessons in the class-room, with the natural consequence that drawing was one of only two subjects in which he got less than top marks in his examinations. Russian language, ironically, was the other.

'Certainly drawing was one of his passions, and the Theatre was another. The Russian Theatre was only a few yards from the school, and we often went there together to see a play or an opera, and at the end of the performance he usually ran home to draw cartoons of the performers. Sometimes we presented plays at school, and I recall particularly young Eisenstein's success in Schiller's *Wallenstein*. He played a woman's part, and it suited both his voice and his physical appearance.

Eisenstein as a child

'He left Riga in 1915, and by then the First World War had already begun. He went as a student to the Institute of Civil Engineering, as he had planned, but in the end, as the world knows, his passion for drama and the visual arts conquered his enthusiasm for engineering. Very few of our classmates survived the World War and the Civil War, and I saw hardly any of them afterwards. It was many years later that I discovered that my school friend Sergei Eisenstein had become a famous film director, and there are those in many countries who used the word "genius" to describe him.'

Another of Eisenstein's childhood friends, who later became a close colleague in both the theatre and the cinema, and one of the most respected actors in the Soviet Union, was Maxim Strauch. Their first meeting was in the garden of a boarding-house, by the seaside and on the outskirts of Riga, which their fathers had rented for the summer. It was in 1908, when Eisenstein was ten years old and his parents had already been estranged for three years:

An apartment block in Riga designed by Eisenstein's father

The Eisenstein family, with friends. Sergei is the boy with the straw hat, his father is standing in uniform, and his mother is the second from the left

Eisenstein with
his mother and father

'What I saw in that garden was a boy with a huge forehead and close-cropped hair, bent over a table and drawing something in a very fat exercise book. I soon learnt that this unusual boy was never idle, but always busy creating something. He spent hour after hour sketching or writing, and the lumber-room was filled to overflowing with his exercise books. Yet he never looked like some sort of child prodigy, pushed reluctantly beyond his strength, and even his appearance was in some way unchildlike. When I first knew him he was already top of the class, and he remained there for the rest of his time at school. Not only, at that age of ten, was he fluent in three languages, but he read the classics in the original with as much ease as in later life he lectured in Berlin in German, at the Sorbonne in French, and in London in English.

'Moreover he had already become a director; not yet for the stage or in the film studio, but in the boarding-house garden. As I was already stage-struck myself in a very small way – I was only eight at the time – I encouraged him. Many boys, in many countries and in many periods of history, have fought battles with toy soldiers, but our battles were probably unique, and their quality was of Eisenstein's making rather than my own. Together we built fortresses and castles, but it was Eisenstein who designed the tiny sets, dressed the troops in battle dress, and at the age of ten directed miniature crowd scenes in that Riga garden which today I could easily connect with some of the sequences in *October* or *Alexander Nevsky* or *Ivan the Terrible*.

'We were very close in those days, as indeed we remained for the rest of his life, and even in 1908 he was an unusual child. By nature he was never particularly frank except to a few of his dearest friends, and he was both lonely and shy, conditions of personality which probably owed a great deal to his parents' separation, and to the fact that his arrogant father was both too busy and too disinclined to spend much time with his only son. It was this very loneliness that both made him shy and yet at the same time forced him into forms of activity which were curiously conspicuous. Despite his personality, it was impossible for him *not* to do the things he knew he could do so well.

'His sense of drama, reflected by the way he manoeuvred our toy soldiers, increased every year. Every summer we would stay together by the seaside, and compare notes on all the plays and operas and circus

A page of Eisenstein's teenage diary

The First World War. A drawing by Eisenstein in 1915

performances that each of us had seen since our last meeting. Although he sometimes visited St Petersburg, where his mother lived, he never went to Moscow, which was my own home city, and so I had the advantage when it came to discussing the latest theatrical events there. I remember beginning one of our summers in Riga with a wildly enthusiastic account of Stanislavsky's production of *The Blue Bird* by Maurice Maeterlinck. I must have been a tolerable actor, because he got so excited that he insisted on an immediate production of the play by Eisenstein and Strauch! He allowed me to direct the performance as long as he could choose his own part. I agreed and he chose, pro-phetically, the role of Fire. Later, to make matters even, he directed me in the youthful Eisenstein–Strauch version of Gogol's *The Marriage*.

'I would hate to give the impression that he behaved purely by instinct and inspiration, for his father, whatever his failures in other directions, taught him one thing that remained with him always – the many merits of the engineer. If things usually seemed easier for him than for the rest of us, it was largely because of this quality of prepared-ness. If few things went wrong it was because so few things were left to chance, and if genius is really, or at least partly, "the infinite capacity for taking pains", then Eisenstein was a genius indeed, and those toy soldiers in that Riga garden would bear witness to the fact.'

The pattern of Eisenstein's life seems already set: the mastery of languages; the talent as a visual artist; the instinct for satire; the passion for the theatre; the engineer's belief in the need for pre-planning, and the merits of construction; the lonely child, victim of incompatible parents, who was certainly bullied and yet ignored by one of them and probably flattered and pampered by the other. In retro-spect he himself came to believe that his silent protest against the tyranny of his father made it easier for him to slide into social protest later on:

'My father was as much of a household despot as that old man, Père Grandet, in Balzac's novel.

'The reasons why I came to support social protest had little to do with the real miseries of social injustice, or material privations, or the zigzags of the struggle for life, but directly and completely from what is surely the prototype of every social tyranny – the father's despotism in a family, which is also a survival of the basic despotism of the head of the "tribe" in every primitive society.'

If that statement is true, then Eisenstein's reaction to his father was ultimately an extremely constructive one, resulting in works of 'social protest' whose quality will be recognized for as long as the cinema is itself regarded as an art form. Far less constructive was the effect of another of his father's characteristics, a chronic form of pedantry that in the son's case was reflected by a tendency in later life, as John Grierson put it, to 'produce numerous theories about all kinds of minute and unimportant aspects of his own work . . . and in his curious habit of guarding all his notes, all his photographs, every drawing and every diagram, both preserving and creating his reputation as ferociously as he ever made his films'.

Circus drawings, 1942

Eisenstein's love of the circus also dated from his childhood, and this was another enthusiasm that he shared with his father – but with one important difference: 'I have adored clowns since I was in my cradle. My father also adored the circus, but what attracted him most of all was what he used to call "high class equestrianship". So I carefully concealed my passion for clowns and pretended to be wildly interested in horses.'

He was also 'wildly interested' in books: 'Books are attracted to me. They make a bee-line for me, and stick to me. I have been so fond of them that at last they have begun to reciprocate. In my hands books burst like ripe fruit. Like magic flowers they unfold their petals to show me the vital thought, the suggestive word, the confirming quotation, the decisive illustration.'

That, of course, was in the future but many of the books that Eisenstein read as a child were unexpected choices for a schoolboy in the Riga of that time. By the age of fourteen he had read most of the works of Dumas, Racine, Corneille and Mallarmé. At sixteen he was given Mignet's *History of the French Revolution* by his father, and successfully demanded sets of Shakespeare and Dickens from his mother. He devoured them all, made copious notes, and allowed his appetite to lead him in the direction of Hugo, Zola, Poe, Tolstoy, and Dostoyevsky.

He was an obsessive visitor to the theatre. There were two theatres in Riga, the 'German' and the 'Russian', and he showed an early preference for the Russian drama, properly feeling it to be more realistic and less artificial than the German. But it was at the German theatre that he saw *Snow Maiden* at the age of ten, and *Chantecler* a year later ('I didn't like it at all'). At the Russian theatre he saw not only most of the established 'classics' but several pieces that were less well known. Of Alexis Tolstoy's *Death of Ivan the Terrible*, for example, he wrote, 'I liked this tragedy very much indeed.' But the greatest theatrical experience of his early youth was a performance of Carlo Gozzi's *Turandot* under the direction of one of the greatest producers in the Russian theatre, Fyodor Kommisarzhevsky (Senior): '. . . from this moment the theatre became the subject of my deepest attention, and my fascination with it was essentially an active one.' He was then thirteen years old.

He was equally interested in opera. His first written notes about the theatre were concerned with opera, and the subjects of the wittiest of his series of youthful drawings were performances of *Queen of Spades* and *Carmen*. Of the composers of opera his favourites were Tchaikovsky, Borodin, Suppé and Glinka, and he was even bold enough to stage a performance of one of Glinka's operas in his own home. He wrote the libretto of an original comic opera, and illustrated the text with drawings of the sets and the costumes.

Sketches after an opera performance in Riga, 1915

The cinema, perhaps inevitably in the early years of the century, played a much smaller part in his life than either the theatre or the circus, though he visited Riga's two cinemas, the 'Crystal' and the 'Progress', from time to time, and always with his nurse. In 1913 he wrote of a 'long' film about Fantômas, and in 1915 was 'much impressed' by a film version of *Les Misérables*. He was less excited by another film whose hero was an American spy: 'I hate stories about spies, and my nanny and I left before the end.'

By his late teens he could extend this list of interests and enthusiasms to include his discovery of some of those visual artists for whom he was to retain the deepest admiration throughout his life: da Vinci, Dürer, Hogarth, Goya, and Daumier. With hindsight, and the knowledge of his work not only as a director of films but as a designer of sets and costumes, it is not difficult to trace his affection for the artists of caricature and distortion.

This list of his early experience and excitement has a deeper significance than that of a fascinating catalogue. As we are in childhood, so to a great extent do we remain for the rest of our lives, and the cliché carries more truth in Eisenstein's case than for most of us. His international fame is that of a film director, and yet he could never bring himself to isolate the film, as an art form, from all those other branches of art which had first begun to excite him in Riga, and most of which he was to practise himself with great distinction. He became an author of film scripts, essays, memoirs; his first published work was as a caricaturist in Petrograd at the age of nineteen, he designed the sets and the costumes of many of the plays and films he directed; and he returned to the stage in 1939 to direct, with conspicuous success, *Die Walküre* at the Bolshoi Theatre in Moscow. His knowledge of the science of engineering, and his general respect for the scientific attitude, remained a constant spine in the centre of his freely imaginative work.

All those factors have been reflected in the comments of his colleagues and friends. Of all the creative artists whose work he knew and respected, the one he most consistently admired was Leonardo da Vinci, and it was of Leonardo that he himself reminded so many of those who knew him.

'Eisenstein was one of those many-sided people of whom there are so few nowadays. He was a sort of Renaissance man, a Leonardo da Vinci, a scientist as well as an artist.' (*Ivor Montagu*)

'When a great man lives close to you, you often fail to appreciate his greatness. Now, so many years after his death, I am absolutely convinced that Eisenstein was a Leonardo da Vinci of the twentieth century.' (*Grigori Rostotsky*)

'The historical figure closest to Eisenstein is, in my opinion, Leonardo da Vinci.' (*Maxim Strauch*)

All of which may read like posthumous flattery, the 'party line' so frequently produced by close friendship. Yet Eisenstein himself seemed to go out of his way to establish the 'Leonardo connection'. Herbert Marshall, one of his pupils at the Moscow Institute of Cinematography in the 1930s, recalls 'an Eisenstein cinémontage breakdown of Leonardo's "The Last Supper" which was part of an exercise he gave to his class'. Professor Marshall has also described Eisenstein's teaching methods in these words:

'The thing that most impressed me was his incredible erudition. He knew several languages and spoke them fluently. His reading, and his extraordinary mind, grasped the whole of world culture. Indeed I would risk suggesting that being in Eisenstein's class must have been like being in the class of Lord Rutherford or Sigmund Freud. His multiplicity constantly amazed me; I knew that I was in the presence of a genius. He would say to us, "I am only incidentally a film-maker, a producer of plays, an artist, a designer, a writer, a lecturer, and so on. My main aim is to do what Darwin did in Natural Science, or what Karl Marx did in the field of Political Economy. I want to lay bare the essential nature of artistic creation." So what he taught his students was not just the making of films; it was an attempt to give us the philosophy of art, of which the cinema is only a part.'

The same point was made by Eisenstein's friend and colleague in Moscow, Mikhail Romm:

'Eisenstein was unusually versatile, a script-writer as well as a director, and a teacher as well as a thinker. He was also a writer of books, a professional scholar, a politician, and a social worker. I am never sure which of those interests came first for him, but I am inclined to think that his work as a film director was not really his main work. He was interested in the theory of direction, but only as part of the more general theory of aesthetics, and it was this which occupied him for so many years. It was a piece of research without an end, to which he dedicated most of his life, and at the centre of it was an examination of Man's behaviour in art – which explains his enormous and constant interest in psychology and the earliest evidence of the creative spirit of mankind. Therefore he studied cultural history in depth, and had a profound knowledge of most of the primitive religions.

'Whatever he did he took seriously, and it was always a great experience to hear him speak of any current piece of research. It is also true to say – and essential that it is said – that however serious he was about anything, he never lost his sense of irony. His eyes were always laughing, and you had to listen extremely carefully to everything he said in case you missed a hidden, and probably very caustic, meaning. And of course everybody who knew him well says the same thing: that he was always working, by day and night, from dawn to dusk and beyond them both. He was either writing, or reading, or preparing a lecture, or writing on a film. Always.'

Eisenstein's knowledge of so many of the great works of art in every form, and his respect for the scientific achievements of his own time, were accepted facts, and there are few people with greater personal experience of this particular phenomenon than Grigori Alexandrov, his close colleague during the most creative period of his life, and who travelled widely with him, not only in their own country, but in Western Europe, the USA and Mexico.

'Whenever I was with Eisenstein abroad, I was constantly being surprised, despite the fact that we had already been friends for several years, by his enormous erudition, and by the depth and width of his culture. At every new meeting he gave proof of his academic knowledge, not boastfully or ostentatiously, but quite naturally, and always with an enormous enthusiasm. If he spoke with a scientist, he knew that man's science. If he spoke with a writer, he knew the writer's work. When we met Edison in the United States, he seemed to know all his inventions. When we met James Joyce in Paris he knew *Ulysses* well and had his own stimulating comments to make on it; when he met George Bernard Shaw in England he shared the author's knowledge of all his plays. This talent of his was no secret, and wherever we went it seemed that all the most famous artists – painters, novelists, poets, dramatists – wanted to meet Sergei Eisenstein. In Berlin he met Tagore, Pirandello, Stefan Zweig, and Lion Feuchtwanger. In Paris he met Léger, Cocteau, Joyce, Aragon, Marinetti, and René Clair; and in Belgium he met James Ensor. Most significantly of all, Sigmund Freud went to a great deal of personal inconvenience to arrange a meeting with Eisenstein.

'Always, and wherever he went, he would be reading. There was never a day in which he did not buy a book, and never a day passed when he failed to receive a book through the post. He wrote for books to every country, and from every country his friends happily and immediately sent them to him. I have always felt that one of the best general courses for students anywhere in the world would be to examine Eisenstein's personal library, carefully and in detail, not only reading his books but also, and more importantly, studying all the thousands of notes that he was always making in them.'

Sixty years after their first meeting by the seaside in Riga, Maxim Strauch sat in the Moscow apartment where Eisenstein's widow, Pera Attasheva, spent her last years, surrounded by his books and the souvenirs of his travels, and said this:

'I always think that a man's house is a good indication of his character, and this apartment inevitably reminds me of the surroundings in which Eisenstein himself used to live. I came to see him very often, but it would be dishonest to claim that whenever I did so I had the sense of entering a private flat. It was more like a library, or a museum, or perhaps even a bookshop, than any kind of domestic nest. Everywhere there were books, and books, and more books. Moreover it was a working library, and all those books had markers, notes, and pieces of paper stuck between the most relevant pages. I always maintain that Eisenstein worked for twenty-four hours every day. When he went to bed he invariably put a notebook beside the bed, and in the morning that notebook was usually full. He never hesitated to phone you at two or three in the morning if he thought you could answer a question that was in his mind at the time. So his flat was not so much a home as a workshop.'

At the age of seventeen Eisenstein registered as a student at the Institute of Civil Engineering in Petrograd. This was certainly the wish of his father, who had once studied there himself, but the decision was taken without reluctance or resistance, and indeed young Eisenstein was later to admit that his intention at that time was to follow in his father's footsteps and become an engineer. It was the Revolution, so he claimed several years later, that forced him to change his mind:

'The Revolution gave me the most precious thing in life – it made an artist out of me. If it had not been for the Revolution I would never have broken the tradition, handed down from father to son, of becoming an engineer. I had the urge to become an artist, but it was the whirlwind of the October Revolution that gave me the one thing that really mattered – the freedom to decide for myself. The Revolution introduced me to art, and art, in its own turn, brought me to the Revolution. So that another thing that the Revolution gave me was the *idea content* of art.'

The urge to become an artist, and especially to work in the theatre, had become more persistent during his period as a student in Petrograd, where the opportunities were much greater than they had ever been in Riga. Now he was in the home city of so many of Russia's most creative artists: Dostoyevsky, Gogol, Turgenev, Pushkin. There were two Leonardos in the Art Gallery which moved him beyond measure, there was the circus and, of course, the theatre. A performance of Lermontov's play *Masquerade*, produced at the Alexandrinsky Theatre and directed by Meyerhold, remained for ever in his memory, and was one of the reasons why he finally chose the theatre as his profession. Yet there was a real sense in which the Revolution of 1917 did in truth give him that precious 'freedom to decide'. With most of his fellow students he volunteered in 1918 to fight for the Red Army in the Civil War, and it was during his period of military service that he found the opportunity to design and direct public performances – including productions of Gogol's *The Gamblers*, and *The Fourteenth of July* by Romain Rolland. In this way he continued to satisfy both his artistic ambition and his social conscience, the latter being fed at the age of seven by the skirmishings in Riga on the occasion of the Revolution of 1905, and by his own more recent familiarity with the events of 1917 in Petrograd: the fall of the Tsar, the rise and fall of Kerensky, and the capture of the Winter Palace by the Bolsheviks. With memories of his father's tyranny, as well as his reading in childhood of Danton and Robespierre, Dumas, Dickens, and Hugo, the decision to go along with his fellow students was probably an easy one, nor is there any reason to believe that he ever regretted it. He became a Soviet artist in 1918, and remained one until he died thirty years later. His break with his parents was now complete, morally, socially, and physically. His mother had already emigrated to France, and his father, after formally joining the 'White Army', was soon to leave for Berlin, where he died in 1921.

In the autumn of 1920 Eisenstein was demobilized. He had already decided to make his career in Moscow rather than Petrograd, for it was clear that in the new Russia Moscow would be the artistic as well as the political centre. He made no attempt to continue his studies in engineering, but chose instead to enrol as a student in the Department of Oriental Languages of the General Staff Academy, a preference less strange than it sounds, because he had already developed a passionate interest in the arts of Japan and had spent several weeks of his spare time as a soldier in learning to speak and write the Japanese language. Yet he never in fact became a formal student of oriental languages, and the reason was an accidental encounter in the entrance hall of a Moscow theatre with his childhood friend, Maxim Strauch:

'In 1914 Eisenstein and I had been separated by the war, and for several years had completely lost sight of each other. Then, in November 1920, we met in Moscow, on an occasion that was very strange, very funny, and full of importance for both of us. It happened at the entrance to the Kamerny Theatre, whose company was working at that time under the outstanding director Alexander Tairov. I very much wanted to see his latest production, but in those days it was extremely hard to get tickets. I had begun to bargain for a seat with a middle-aged ticket-tout when I suddenly had the sensation that someone was watching me from behind. I turned round, and indeed there was a man staring at me, very intently too, and with great concentration. I said to the ticket-tout: "Let's move on, I think we've been spotted." So we walked to another part of the foyer, and continued our somewhat irregular negotiations. After a minute or so I turned round again, and the man was still there, and still watching me. In the end he walked boldly up to me and said, very quietly, "Aren't you Strauch?" It was Eisenstein! I hadn't recognized him because he had just arrived in Moscow from the Front, and he still wore his service greatcoat. We both began to bargain for tickets, and we were both successful. Then, after the performance, we spent the rest of the night walking and talking in the Boulevard, and it was obvious after only a few minutes that we had both been swept off our feet by the theatre as a profession and by the Revolution that had so completely changed our country. So, in our youthful enthusiasm – he was nearly twenty-three years old and I was only twenty – we decided to work in a new form of theatre. What happened was that we joined what was really the very first genuine "workers" theatre; the "Proletkult".'

Moscow's Proletkult Theatre had its headquarters in the lush home of a Tsarist millionaire who had imported it stone by stone from Portugal, and it was here that Eisenstein was accepted as a set designer. He was given the chance to practise his theories and ideas in an atmosphere far more stimulating than the seaside at Riga or the occasional performance by a group of the Red Army, and Moscow, in the years immediately after the Revolution, was indeed one of the most exciting cities in the world. All things seemed possible except housing, food, and clothing; not only was it 'great to be alive' in that particular dawn, but it must have been 'very heaven' to be twenty-three years old. For the young intellectuals of the day Russia was the home of the best artists and scientists in Europe: Pavlov and Timiryazev were honoured scientists, and among the writers were Babel, Gorky, Mayakovsky and Pasternak. The greatest figure in the new Soviet

Eisenstein, first from the left, in Moscow in 1923 with the poets Boris Pasternak (on extreme left) and Vladimir Mayakovsky (on extreme right)

theatre was indisputably Vsevolod Meyerhold, whose production of *Masquerade* had so profoundly impressed the young Eisenstein in Petrograd. Eisenstein and Strauch were just two of the dozens of young men and women who chose the revolutionary theatre as a profession. Another was Sergei Yutkevich who was also to shift his career from the stage to the screen and is particularly qualified to write of Eisenstein's work at that time:

'Eisenstein's first job as a designer for the Proletkult was for two plays with the artist Nikolai Nikitin, which went largely unnoticed. Then, and surprisingly early in his career, came the production that made him famous over-night – though still within a fairly narrow artistic circle – an adaptation of Jack London's story *The Mexican*. The producer was a member of the famous Moscow Arts Theatre, Valeri Smishlayev, and Eisenstein was officially the designer of the sets and the costumes. But it was Eisenstein who really created the entire production. It was typical of him not to be satisfied with a subsidiary function, and it was impossible for him to do anything less than think out the production in its entirety; by which I mean that he worked out the director's interpretation and applied it in a manner wholly typical of that extraordinary young man named Eisenstein.

'The plot of *The Mexican* is concerned with two rival boxing managers, and Eisenstein's visual treatment of this rivalry was extremely original. He made the office of one of the managers circular and the other square. So Stage Right was shaped as a circle and Stage Left as a square, and this stylization applied to the actors' costumes as well as to the lay-out of the stage. On Stage Left the cast had square heads and wore square, chequered costumes, and on Stage Right they were all circular. But this revolutionary idea was not the main point of the production, for the central moment of the play was a boxing match that took place "off-stage" while the visible cast merely reacted to it. Or rather this was true of the play on the written page, but it was unacceptable to Eisenstein. Instead, he transformed the boxing match into the focal point of the entire piece, placing a boxing-ring downstage and as close to the audience as possible. This device of making a sporting event which really took place – or very nearly, for it was played with total realism by Grigori Alexandrov as one of the boxers and by a genuine boxer as the other – into a popular theatrical "show" was an idea that completely captured the theatre public of Moscow.

'In the autumn of 1921 Eisenstein and I were both accepted into the famous "directors' workshop" run by the man who was our god and idol in those days, Vsevolod Meyerhold, and I still remember the occasion a month or so later when Eisenstein risked taking his new teacher, and all the students as well, to see *The Mexican*. Fortunately Meyerhold was very impressed, perhaps because the production was extremely close to his own conception of the modern theatre, of which he was indisputably the leading figure at that time. He was delighted to have Eisenstein as one of his students, and at the end of the first term asked him to design a production of *Puss in Boots*, by the nineteenth-century German dramatist Ludwig Tieck. Once again Eisenstein's interpretation was completely original. He exchanged the auditorium with the stage, so that when the curtain rose – or, rather, when the performance began, for there was no curtain in the literal sense – the audience seemed to be looking at a second auditorium, and the stage itself was seen from the "wings".

'During the same period Eisenstein conceived and made a model set for a production of George Bernard Shaw's *Heartbreak House*, which Meyerhold was planning for his own theatre. Shaw himself had suggested that the house in his play should resemble a ship, and Eisenstein, taking the hint, designed his own set in terms of a ship; but a modern ship, not an old one. The most interesting point about this set, on which the actors could move both vertically and horizontally, was a large striped divan in the form of a semi-circle which was placed at the back of the stage, and on which the actors rested whenever they had finished each particular piece of the play. They went into action on the spot, and at no time did they leave the playing area. The "wings", with their familiar function as places of exits and entrances, were therefore abolished. The model, which happily has been preserved, has always seemed to me to be a beautiful solution to one of the problems of the stage.

'Eisenstein's work in the theatre between 1920 and 1923 was by no means confined to the Proletkult and to Meyerhold. He also worked for a "Workshop Theatre" run by Foregger – a former German baron –

who happened to share his interest in the circus and the Commedia dell'Arte, and was himself experimenting in the use of masks. He refused to "stylize" them in the manner of the Commedia dell'Arte, or of the old popular theatre of France, and instead chose his masks from contemporary life, so that one might be a girl communist, another a poet, a third an intellectual philosopher, and a fourth a city merchant. He transferred to the stage many of his observations of real life, and a

Stage design for a production of *Heartbreak House*, 1922

great part of the action and the dialogue was improvised by the cast on the spot. Looking back from this distance of time I find that it reminds me very much of what nowadays we call a "happening", and our young directors sometimes behave as though the whole conception is new and revolutionary. Every generation rediscovers what has been discovered already, and the true inventors of the "happening" were probably Foregger and Eisenstein.

Costume design for *Heartbreak House*, 1922

'The last evening of 1921 was the opening of Eisenstein's biggest success with Foregger's company, a piece called *Good Relations with Horses* by Vladimir Mass. This was a highly original mixture of Foregger's faith in the contemporary comedy with masks, and the "variety show" or Music Hall, and Eisenstein showed a superb ingenuity in designing the costumes to match his extremely witty ideas. There is one particular costume that I remember very vividly – a satirical reflection of a fashionable "school" of poets called the "Imagists". The "Imagists" were divided into two opposing groups: the first of them claimed to represent the peasants and the countryside, and the second group spoke for those who lived in the cities. Both groups and points of view were reflected in the costume that Eisenstein designed for a character called "Poet", which he divided into two conflicting halves, a peasant with shirt and trousers in typical "peasant style", and a gentleman of "the city" with an extremely misshapen frock coat. The costumes for the play completely conveyed the essence of the characters, and the women's costumes were especially original in their inventiveness. Eisenstein's basic technique with these costumes was to make a very light circle of wire, which he then covered with ribbons. In that way he allowed himself to display the artistes' legs.

'A month after the first performance of *Good Relations with Horses* Eisenstein designed the sets and costumes for another of Foregger's productions, an old melodrama called *The Kidnapper*, and this time he took as his inspiration one of his favourite painters, Daumier. He worshipped Daumier and later, when he travelled to France, he bought as many of Daumier's lithographs as he could find.

'In April 1922 he and I were asked to design the sets of *Macbeth* for another group – the Central Theatre of Enlightenment, whose producer was Tikhonovich. The first thing we did was to make a model, for we both preferred models to sketches, and I still regard that *Macbeth* as one of the most original ideas of Eisenstein's short career in the theatre, and in stating that belief I am of course also conceding that it was essentially his inspiration rather than my own. Inevitably it was a single set and, also inevitably, there was no curtain. Up Stage Centre there was a throne, a symbol of the power that Macbeth hoped to capture for himself. In the right-hand corner there was a vast cage that Eisenstein used for a variety of purposes; as the entrance to a

Costume design for the First Murderer in *Macbeth*, 1921

castle, as a rampart, as the porter's closet. Even the murderers came
out of it. Our set was in a uniform shade of grey, which we covered
with canvas and touched up very slightly in black. The only noticeable
colour was in the costumes, which were in red and gold. I think we
must confess to the undoubted influence on us of Gordon Craig, but it
still remains fair to say that *Macbeth* was essentially an original design
for a play by Shakespeare, and executed almost entirely by Eisenstein.

'In the autumn of 1922 he was appointed Artistic Director of a
newly founded branch of the original Proletkult theatre known as "The
Strolling Players". For them he designed and directed *Enough Folly in
a Wise Man* by Alexander Ostrovsky, and *Listen Moscow!* by Sergei
Tretyakov. *A Wise Man* is generally regarded as the most remarkable
of all the productions in the Moscow theatre during that particularly
exciting period, and largely because Eisenstein removed completely any
sense of scenic illusion, relying instead on all the established principles
of one of his most favourite of all the dramatic arts – the circus. The
only "props" used in *A Wise Man* were those from the circus, and it is
probably true to say that Eisenstein carried the principles of the circus
to their logical and satirical conclusion. The band played jazz – quite
a daring thing in revolutionary Moscow – and Alexandrov walked the
tight-rope in his bare feet.

'Eisenstein's last production was *Gas Masks*, another of Tretyakov's
plays, and this time he left the physical theatre altogether and took his
actors into a real gas works, where the play is set. The audience sat on
rows of wooden benches placed round part of the factory floor. It was
not by any means a complete success, but its importance lies in the fact
that Eisenstein had moved from the unreal circus-like atmosphere of
A Wise Man to the naturalistic and "documentary" setting of a real
factory. The theatre, so it seemed, had become too small for him, and
he had already begun his journey into the cinema.

'There are two further points I should make about his career in the
theatre, and the first of them relates directly to those principles of
"montage" for which he became so famous later on. It is what he
called his "theory of focal points", which in English has often been
described as "the montage of attractions",[1] the aim being to "attract"
the audience (and now and then to pulverize it or smash an artistic
fist in its face) by a carefully planned sequence of "focal points", of

which the boxing match in *The Mexican* is an obvious example. As a theory it shows both the careful planning of the engineer (the "focal points" are chosen with the precision of a slide-rule) and the sudden inspiration of the creative artist (the exact nature of each "focal point" being often decided in detail by the urge of the moment). There can be no success without planning, but planning itself is fruitless unless it has an ultimate artistic purpose.

'My last point has nothing whatever to do with either the theatre or the cinema, but is the social fact that all those rare and exciting experiments in so many Moscow theatres took place at the end of a Civil War and in a city on the verge of starvation. There were many days when we were lucky if we found two loaves of bread. The winters were cold, and so were the theatres, and very few of us could boast of more than a single battered suit. Eisenstein was neither rich, nor well-fed, nor well-clothed. It is a background too easily taken for granted, or forgotten, but it makes his enthusiasm as well as his artistic achievements all the more remarkable.'

2

Revolution on the Screen

Grigori Kozintsev, director of the Russian film versions of *Hamlet* and *King Lear*, had this to say about his senior contemporary, Sergei Eisenstein:

'In Eisenstein's case the most important thing to consider is not so much his place in the history of the contemporary cinema, but in the history of modern culture as a whole. To say that Eisenstein was one of the greatest film directors of our time is to say something both very obvious and very little. I believe myself that he was essentially an investigator, in search of an art form that had not yet been created, and his films were just the first steps in the development of that art. Nor in his own lifetime did he succeed in realizing what had inspired his heart and his mind.

'He began his work in films at a time when the cinema was simply a new form of entertainment, and his dream was to turn the screen into an instrument of shock. His intention was not to provide the public with an amiable pastime, a pleasant way of spending an hour or two, but to dive headlong into the hard and stormy history of our own time. He was the first director to demonstrate that the subject-matter of this new art of cinematography can be much more than the telling of a personal story. On the contrary, in its magnitude it can be the essential history of an age, and the true heroes of Eisenstein's films were masses of people – crowds on the streets in their thousands, a fleet of battleships with their crews, and some of those events which are known to have changed the face of history. This indeed is what he had at the back of his mind when he spoke of directing a film version of Karl Marx's *Das Kapital*.

'Fundamental to all his work was the element of shock, or at least surprise, though I myself suspect that the "shock-screen" of his dreams was only partly realized in his own films. Yet this is much less important than the fact that he left us not only the films themselves, and his extraordinary articles on film theory, but also those first glimpses of a new art that has been achieved only very occasionally so far.

'I find myself thinking of Eisenstein's vision when I watch the films of other and more recent directors. When I saw Ingmar Bergman's *Persona*, for example, I said to myself, "But this is surely what Eisenstein tried vainly to do in Hollywood forty years ago!" I can hardly believe that Bergman consciously stole something from Eisenstein, and indeed he probably had no knowledge at all of what Eisenstein was trying to do in that place at that time. These influences and ambitions are very hard to describe in words, but I would say that there was "something in the air", and that Eisenstein was the first man to see it. Or, to be more exact, to "foresee" it. It is for this reason, so I personally believe, that the art which Eisenstein used to dream about will one day be truly realized, and then only will we be able to recognize him as perhaps the greatest innovator in the entire culture of the twentieth century.'

Eisenstein is such a household name for students of the cinema that it is too easy to forget the minute size of his output as a film-maker, and the very few years into which it was concentrated. In twenty-two years he completed only seven films, and four of them were made in a period of four and a half years: *Strike*, the first of them, had its Moscow première in February 1925 and the fourth (*Old and New*) in the autumn of 1929. When at the World's Fair in Brussels in 1958 an international jury of over a hundred film critics and historians voted *Battleship Potemkin* as the best film ever made, they were honouring a work that was completed in four months and was only the second film of a young director whose age at that time was twenty-seven.

His first experience as a film-maker was not in fact for the cinema at all, but a short sequence shown as part of the stage production of *A Wise Man*. From the brief segment that still survives it was clearly as non-naturalistic and as circus-like as the 'live' parts of the play. The actors –

among them Grigori Alexandrov, Maxim Strauch, Mikhail Gomorov, and Eisenstein himself – wore either masks or heavily stylized make-up, and at the end of it Alexandrov, as the character called Glumov whose diary was the theme of the entire sequence, climbs to a high roof and jumps off. In the performance at the Proletkult he then burst through the screen and on to the stage. It was a good example of Eisenstein's shock tactics with his audience.

It was *A Wise Man* that first brought Eisenstein into professional contact with one of the most remarkable, and also one of the most under-rated, figures in the Soviet cinema, Lev Kuleshov:

'The first time I met Eisenstein was after his production of *A Wise Man* in 1923, a theatrical event that impressed me as much as every-body else. Here was a theatre director who used new methods, and who seemed to be speaking to us with those new words for which we were all waiting, and not always patiently, in those stormy and passionate years.

'Together he and I made a business arrangement. I was at that time in charge of a film "workshop" – it was generally known as "Kuleshov's Laboratory" – in the first Soviet State School of Cinematography. Our intentions were entirely admirable, but our accommodation was totally inadequate, whereas Eisenstein had superb accommodation in the building of the Proletkult. Hence our business agreement, whereby Eisenstein gave my own students the use of his floor-space for their gymnastics, sport, acrobatics and so forth, and in return I gave lectures on the cinema to his actors.

'We both gained from our collaboration, and in Eisenstein's case the gain was largely due to his comparative ignorance of the cinema. Yet he had already developed a great interest in it, and his appetite had been increased by his experience in making that short sequence for *A Wise Man*. So he decided to study the cinema in earnest, and he asked if he might join my "laboratory" as an observer. I agreed at once, with the consequence that for three months, and regularly each evening, he worked with me on the technique of film editing, and especially the editing of the subject-matter that attracted him most of all – mass movement and mass action. Unfortunately everything had to be done on paper. There was very little film-stock in Moscow in those days, and hardly any at all for courses like mine.

'Eisenstein proved to be a most extraordinary student, and I can say in all sincerity that in those three months he completely mastered all that was known at that time about the arts and techniques of the cinema. He began as my pupil, but very soon he became my teacher, thereby proving the truth of one of his own favourite sayings: that anyone in the world could learn to become a film director, but some people needed three years' training and others at least three hundred years. For Sergei Eisenstein the time required was exactly three months – part-time!

'Later, when film-stock became more readily available – though we must remember that there was a constant shortage throughout the 1920s – Soviet film production inevitably increased, and in 1924 Eisenstein was given the chance to make his first full-length film, *Strike*. It was a particularly interesting film because of the superb editing of the scenes of mass action, proving that our evenings together had been anything but a waste of time. It was also typical of Eisenstein's early work in having no individual heroes, but being packed with big 'occasions'' and vast crowd scenes. There had been nothing at all like it in the previous history of the Russian cinema, and its revolutionary subject-matter was also new. So when *Strike* was first shown to the public, Eisenstein once again became the immediate centre of critical attention, but this time in the cinema and not in the theatre.'

Strike was set up by Goskino, the Soviet Union's first state production group, in collaboration with the Proletkult, and the names of many of Eisenstein's colleagues from the theatre appear in the screen credits. Grigori Alexandrov, for example, was credited three times, as an assistant director, as one of the authors of the script, and as an actor playing the part of a foreman. Mikhail Gomorov played one worker and Alexander Antonov, also of the Proletkult, was another. Maxim Strauch also worked on the production. Particularly significant was the recruitment as principal cameraman of Eduard Tisse, who had been recommended by the head of Goskino, Boris Mikhin. Tisse not only photographed *Strike* with superb imagination but remained to work on every film that Eisenstein directed, and today there can be few professional camermen who would deny that he was the greatest of them all.

Strike is a film which perfectly illustrates two of Eisenstein's principles, and the first of them is reflected in one of his own favourite reflections: 'Biologically we are all mortal, but we become immortal in what we achieve for society – in those contributions we make towards carrying the torch of social progress from one generation to the next.' The second principle was this: 'The films I make are never "film eyes" but always "film fists". I never make films in which the camera is an "objective witness", to be watched by an impassive eye of glass. I prefer

Strike, 1925. The workers are beaten up by the Tsar's mounted troops

to hit people hard on the nose.' It was a reaction to the contemporary work of Dziga Vertov, who made 'news' films without any comment, implied or stated, in the belief that the sole function of the camera is to record whatever it happens to see. *Strike*, on the contrary, was a committed work both in conception and in execution, originally intended as part of a cycle of films concerned with the history of the working-class movement in Russia. In *Strike* the workers are handled for the most part naturalistically, whereas the capitalist bosses and their agents are often held up to ridicule, for it was Eisenstein's habit to poke fun at those he disliked. As a film it suffers from a mixture of styles. Several sequences, like the famous scene in which the factory workers are beaten up by the mounted forces of the Tsar, are totally realistic, and others, such as those concerned with the spies employed by the factory owners, rely on the familiar techniques of the circus. To this extent *Strike* is a logical extension of Eisenstein's approach to the theatre, showing the same enthusiasms and the same fundamental principles. It is totally typical of his work, and could have been made by no other director, and the point has been well made by his friend Ivor Montagu:

'Two aspects of Eisenstein's career are apparent in every foot of *Strike*. On the one hand, here and there, actual material is arranged with economy into a realism poignant in its universality; on the other, the fantastic clowning of the circus shows itself in detail everywhere, and in the exaggerated, even hypertrophied, treatment of particular episodes and the plot in general. The twisting of actual material, with an ironic air of naturalism, to express such fanciful, exaggerated "propaganda-poster" ideas, works often with a confusing, indeed shattering, effect on the spectator that must have delighted young Eisenstein and flung him passionately in love with the film medium and its potentialities.'[1]

This confusion of styles produced a varied response from the original audience in 1925, and although *Strike* was vigorously praised by the critics of *Pravda*, *Izvestia*, and *Kino-Gazeta*, its strong passages of naturalism seem to have been easier for the general public to digest than those sequences whose origins were the circus and the theatre of satire. It is also, in many of its sequences, an extremely cruel film: the workers are beaten up in a scene of unsparing realism as their children are thrown down by their attackers from the heights of a tenement block. Cruelty is a constant factor in Eisenstein's films, and whatever its deep causes may have been within himself, he could always produce its intellectual justification. In the case of *Strike* he claimed to have been directly influenced by his memory of the 1905 revolution in Riga when, at the age of seven, he had himself seen the barricades and the repression of the workers. 'Cruelty', he wrote many years later, 'is mixed closely with the theme of social injustice and the uprising against it.'

Some of the reservations which the original audience had about *Strike* were to be echoed on a more intellectual level by Eisenstein himself:

'*Strike* . . . brought collective and mass action onto the screen, in contrast to individualism and the "triangle" drama of the bourgeois cinema. . . . No screen had ever before reflected an image of collective action. Now the concept of "collectivity" was to be pictured. But our enthusiasm produced a one-sided representation of the masses and the "collective"; one-sided because "collectivism" means the maximum development of the individual within the "collective", a conception irreconcilably opposed to bourgeois individualism. Our first mass films missed this deeper meaning. Still, I am sure that for its period this deviation was not only natural but necessary. It was important that the screen be first penetrated by the general image, the "collective", the deeper meaning, demanded of cinema today, would have found acceptance almost impossible if the way had not been cleared by the general concept.'[2]

For those in control of Soviet film production in 1925 *Strike* was good enough for Eisenstein to be given his second film, and as it eventually became the work we know as *Battleship Potemkin* this act of faith by his sponsors was magnificently repaid. Once again the credits contain familiar names: Alexandrov, Strauch, Gomorov and Antonov were the director's 'assistants', and of these Alexandrov, Gomorov and Antonov were also among the actors. The cameraman was Eduard Tisse, and Eisenstein credited himself as director, film editor and script-writer. Both Alexandrov and Strauch have spoken at length about the making of *Battleship Potemkin*. Here, first of all, is a statement by Alexandrov:

'The original intention had been to make a film to be called *1905*, with the purpose of showing many of the remarkable events of that early revolutionary year, and Eisenstein was appointed director in March 1925. At once he began to work on a script with Nina Agadzhanova-Shutko, a woman who was both a respected writer and someone who had herself played a part in the events of 1905 as an extremely active member of the Bolshevik Party.

'We had very little time in which to make the film, and by modern standards the timetable given to us was alarmingly short. It was also unavoidable, for a film designed to celebrate the twentieth anniversary of a particular series of historical events should clearly be completed before the end of the anniversary year. That year was 1925, and so in principle we had until 31 December to finish it, or nine months from the day when Eisenstein and Nina Agadzhanova-Shutko first began work on the script. Nor should we forget that the film was originally intended to cover a great many incidents in 1905, and indeed the *Potemkin* affair was a tiny part of the original conception, occupying only two pages of the first scenario.

'Shooting for *1905* began in the early spring, not in Odessa but in Leningrad, and when Agadzhanova was still at work on the script. But the weather was bad, shooting was delayed, and as every day brought us nearer to our dreaded deadline we became more and more anxious. In the end we were advised by the Leningrad experts to go south for a time and work on another sequence for the film in the hope of returning to Leningrad when the weather improved. So we went to Odessa, and set up our headquarters in the Hotel London, where Eisenstein himself wrote the script of what eventually became *Battleship Potemkin*. We never went back to Leningrad.'

To that statement Maxim Strauch adds another fascinating detail:

'Although the *Potemkin* mutiny was originally planned as a short sequence in the long film of *1905* – which of course was never made – there is no doubt that Eisenstein would have found a place for it in his film. I can state this with certainty because I remember very well the night when he came back in enormous excitement from the Lenin Library in Moscow to the flat we shared together at that time. He carried a copy of a magazine published in Paris, called *L'Illustration*, which contained an article about the mutiny, and included a drawing of the famous scene on the steps of Odessa. What happened on those steps – or rather what did *not* happen, for historically the scene is extremely dubious – seemed to Eisenstein to have all the potentialities of a sequence that on a single location could summarize so much of what he wanted to say in his film. So as soon as we were all established in Odessa his very first professional act was to go out and see the steps for himself. They did not disappoint him.'

Another and less familiar eyewitness of the shooting of *Battleship Potemkin* is today a Professor of Physics at the University of Odessa. In 1925 he played the part of the small boy who was shot on the steps, Pavel Alexandrovich Glaubermann:

'The year 1925 was a long time ago, and not even a middle-aged professor can be expected to remember everything that happened to him at the age of five. Had I known that this charming man with hair like an electric shock, and who "discovered" me on the school football field, would one day be described as the greatest film director of his age, then possibly I might today remember a great deal more!

'I was goalkeeper, and Eisenstein chose me for the part because he wanted a boy of my age who could fall convincingly. Perhaps, so it seems to me now, he was really looking for a boy who positively relished the idea of falling. But to fall on a playing-field is one thing, and to fall on the hard Odessa steps is quite another. Anyway he chose me, this man with the bristling hair, and he made me fall for five or six days. I had to fall "well", so they kept telling me. I remember those five or six days, and I remember the little cigarette packet that lay on the particular step where I had to fall. I am not a film man, and I know literally nothing of the techniques of film-making, but at least I now know that in order to end my fall at the proper place in the shot I had to finish on that wretched empty cigarette packet.

'I got an enormous thrill from this dramatic performance, enjoying every minute of it, bruises and all, but bored to distraction whenever they had to reload the camera, or left me alone for an hour or two and went off to shoot something or somebody else. I was so excited that when my falling was over I kept coming back to the steps every day, partly to see what was going on, and also in the secret hope that if I hung about for long enough they might have pity on me and ask me to fall somewhere else. So I came back in this way for another few days, and they were always very kind to me, explaining everything, and telling me exactly what they were up to. They even let me ride on the camera-trolley that travelled on specially built rails beside the vast flight of steps. And the cameraman – the great Eduard Tisse, had I only known it – let me sit hour after hour at the foot of his camera.

'In the end they left the steps, and I went back to the football field and resumed my less spectacular career as a goalkeeper. I liked to think that now I could fall with greater expertise than ever before but, sad to say, I had no idea that I had taken part in one of the greatest film sequences ever to be made, or that my falling would be shown all over the world, and is indeed being shown to this day. Nothing that I might achieve in my chosen profession can ever count as much in the eyes of the world as my genius as a faller on cigarette packets.'

Of another familiar sequence in *Battleship Potemkin* Maxim Strauch had this to say:

'There is one scene in the film which has always been praised as much for Tisse's photography as for Eisenstein's conception, and indeed Eisenstein himself was always extremely fond of it: the sequence of mourning, beautifully shot in the mist of the Black Sea. Again he freely admitted that like the scene on the Odessa Steps it bore little relation to documentary reality. There is no evidence whatever that such an event ever took place in a fog! Nor did the mist appear in the script of *Battleship Potemkin*.

'What happened, quite literally, was this: one morning in Odessa, during the shooting of the film, we all woke up in the Hotel London, which is not very far from the top of the steps and looks out over the harbour, and could see nothing but fog. The Black Sea, a few hundred yards away, was invisible. To film in such weather, with such minimal visibility, was ludicrous. Clearly the only sensible thing to do was to go back to bed and catch up on all our lost sleep. But Eduard Tisse disagreed absolutely, and insisted on shooting. He persuaded a reluctant

Eisenstein that he was right, and they went together down to the harbour, where they made that splendid sequence of the sailors of the *Potemkin* mourning their dead comrade. It would have been a fine scene anyway, but it was infinitely more emotive by the very fact of the fog, adding its own comment to the tragic mood of the mourning.'

Let Grigori Alexandrov complete the story of the making of *Battleship Potemkin*:

'The film which lasts for nearly an hour and a quarter at its original

Eisenstein during the shooting of *Battleship Potemkin*, 1925

length was edited in less than a fortnight by Eisenstein and an assistant, working day and night and hardly ever leaving the cutting-room. The first Moscow performance, a special one in advance of its general public showing, was scheduled for 21 December 1925, and I remember that we spent most of the final days with the man who helped us to arrange the titles, which were always very important in any silent film by Eisenstein – not only the wording, but also the size and style of the lettering, the use of exclamation marks, and so on. We were still working on this on the night of the first screening, which was in the Bolshoi Theatre, and I spent the evening riding on a motor-cycle between the cutting-room and the theatre, carrying the reels one at a time. When Eisenstein was finally happy with the last reel, he sat on the back of my motor-cycle with the can of film under his arm. We had no time to lose because we both knew perfectly well that the performance must have started, but when we were in the middle of Red Square, and about a quarter of a mile from the Bolshoi, the motor-cycle broke down. So we ran the rest of the way! Of course such a situation would be disastrous nowadays, but in 1925 every film was shown on a single projector with

Battleship Potemkin, 1925. The officer diving overboard is G. V. Alexandrov

a break between each reel – and incidentally we constructed our films with those breaks in mind, a fact sometimes forgotten by modern critics. So all was well, except that the break between the last two reels was nearly twenty minutes long!'

None of this, of course, relates directly to the quality of the film itself, though it certainly makes that quality all the more remarkable. *Battleship Potemkin* is shorter than *Strike*, and has a more consistent style. All echoes of the circus have gone and the characters, played by actors and non-actors alike, have the ring of reality, so that the film is essentially a dramatized documentary. It remains so despite the fact that so many of its finest sequences either had no historical basis or were conceived by the inspiration of the moment. There are many examples of this apart from those already given, one of the most famous being the sequence of the marble lion which rises in anger at the events it is apparently watching, an idea that occurred to Eisenstein when, by pure chance, he saw several statues of lions, each in a different physical attitude, at the Alupka Palace in Odessa. It may well be that the success of *Battleship Potemkin* owes a great deal to Eisenstein's reliance on his own inspiration, rather than on the meticulous pre-planning of the mathematician or the engineer. That it was made so quickly is a reason for its sense of spontaneity, almost as though it took no longer to shoot than the time-span of the events it portrayed. The absurdly short editing time must have compelled Eisenstein to make quick, instinctive decisions rather than referee that recurring wrestling-match between his feelings as an artist and his intellectual principles as the film theorist who was trained as an engineer. It is probably unfair, on the other hand, to underestimate the enormous work involved in the original plan for *1905*, which he shared with Agadzhanova, even though her direct contribution to the final film was minimal. Granted the existence on paper of so much of the documentary background of the year 1905, Eisenstein could very well grasp the 'feel' and the spirit of that particular year, and must have known just how far he could go with his inspired and unexpected ideas without destroying that essential spirit. It must be no coincidence that he often professed his agreement with Goethe's belief that 'in order to be truthful you can risk an occasional defiance of truth itself'.

Yet there is a problem here, and it is well illustrated by the general impression of an audience which for fifty years, and almost entirely thanks to Eisenstein, has really believed that the scene on the Odessa Steps is a faithful reconstruction of an actual event. The moment when this artistic 'lie' is made known for what it truly is can also be the moment when faith in the 'truthfulness' of the work as a whole might begin to evaporate. There were sequences in *Strike*, as soon there would be sequences in *October*, which clearly could never have happened as Eisenstein presented them. He knew they were incredible, just as the circus is incredible, and he expected his audience to accept them as such and to enjoy their place in his artistic pattern. Like every true artist in any medium, he was concerned to get from his audience the response he wanted, and to be granted that essential 'suspension of disbelief'. This was no doubt his intention in *Battleship Potemkin*, and it is unfair to blame the artist for the inevitable consequence of his 'naturalistic' technique in that particular film – that his audience, generation after generation, accepts as historic truth all those things that *seem* to be true.

Battleship Potemkin has nevertheless been generally regarded as a masterpiece of the film-maker's art, which indeed it undoubtedly is. Though spontaneously created in many of its details it was also loyal to Eisenstein's consistent beliefs; its editing is loyal to the principle that film-editing should be a 'montage of collisions', it bristles with examples of the theory of 'focal points', and it most certainly contains its fair share of moments when the audience is 'punched on the nose'. Yet its initial reception was extremely mixed. Was it a 'feature film' or was it a 'documentary'? Was it not perhaps too clever in technique to communicate its purpose to a vast and largely 'uneducated' audience? Was it not essentially too emotional and sentimental? To this last criticism Eisenstein had this to say:

'I am accused of making *Battleship Potemkin* too emotional. But are we not all people? Don't we have human feelings? Don't we have passions? Don't we have our own tasks and purposes in life? The film was enormously successful in Berlin, and in other parts of a post-war Europe that was plunged in the chaos of total instability, and at that time and in those places it sounded a clarion call to a life that was worthy of mankind itself. Is not such emotion therefore justified? Should we not be allowed to lift up our heads and feel ourselves to be men? This is what *Battleship Potemkin* is about, no more and no less.'

Having reflected the first Russian revolution it seemed inevitable that Eisenstein should be asked to tackle the second. He began shooting *October* in April 1927, parts of it were shown at a special performance on the tenth anniversary of the Bolshevik Revolution (7 November 1927), and the complete film was released to the general public in March 1928 – though the word 'complete' is inaccurate, as numerous changes had to be made for political reasons, and Grigori Alexandrov has stated that Stalin himself visited the cutting-room on at least one occasion to order the removal of sequences that he felt were sympathetic

October, 1928. Camera position for the attack on the Winter Palace.

to Trotsky, and another which showed Lenin in 'an unsatisfactory light'. On the film's credits Alexandrov appears for the first time as Eisenstein's equal partner as both co-director and co-author of the script. Tisse, who was again the principal cameraman, also played the part of a German soldier, and the assistant directors were Strauch, Gomorov, and Ilya Trauberg. The final version of the film had a length of 2,220 metres, which was 251 metres longer than *Strike* and 480 metres longer than *Battleship Potemkin*.

October also had its sequences of mass action, and the attack on the Winter Palace is as well known to cinema audiences as the slaughter on the steps of Odessa. It may not be as much admired, but at least it was the reconstruction of a real event, and Grigori Alexandrov recalls well how it was done:

'When we filmed the storming of the Winter Palace the headquarters of our unit was underneath the big bronze horses on top of the arch that leads into the square from the main part of the city, and exactly opposite the Palace itself. It was from this position that Eisenstein shouted his orders through a megaphone to the vast crowd that stormed the Palace on our behalf. There were more than 5,000 of them altogether, armed with rifles and blank ammunition, and nearly all of them came from the factories of Leningrad. Many had taken part in the October Revolution of 1917, and had attacked the Winter Palace in reality ten years before. Their job was to do once again what they had done then. So, at the agreed time, our orders went out from beneath those bronze horses, and 3,000 people went into action from the various sides of the square. The rest came running from beneath us, under the arch, heading straight for the Palace.

'In 1917 the real attack had taken place at night and in the dark, and so we filmed at night. But in those days it was very difficult to light a large area, even though we deliberately chose to shoot the sequence in June, during the so-called "White Nights", when in Leningrad you can easily read a newspaper out of doors without artificial light. But the film stock available to us in 1927 was by no means "fast" enough, and for much of the time we were forced to crank the camera more slowly than usual to increase the exposure; which in turn had the effect of unnaturally speeding up the tempo of the crowd movements.

October. The camera position at the entrance to the Square before the Winter Palace. Eisenstein stands behind the camera, Alexandrov is on the left on the rostrum, and Tisse sits below him

'This was a problem we could anticipate and allow for. Other hazards were totally unexpected. For instance, some of those who took part in the sequence had recently returned from the various fronts of the Civil War. They had come home with some of their "live" cartridges, and decided to add to the realism by using them for the filming, so that when it was all over we had difficulty in accounting for some of the windows in the Palace that had been smashed by bullets, and a few of the rare sculptures outside the building that had been chipped by the same cause. We had arranged to explode dummy grenades during our shooting to help the realism of the atmosphere, but compared with the live bullets they were innocence itself. Not surprisingly we had our own genuine casualties, and most of them were caused by badly handled bayonets. Indeed it has long been a joke in the Soviet film industry that more casualties were caused by Eisenstein's storming of the Winter Palace in June 1927 than by the attack of the original Bolsheviks in October 1917.'

Many friends and critics have written about the crowd sequences in Eisenstein's films of the 1920s, which were quite different in essence and spirit from those of his later and 'period' films, *Alexander Nevsky* and *Ivan the Terrible*. For example, John Grierson, who worked on the US version of *Battleship Potemkin* and knew Eisenstein personally, made this comment:

'I believe Eisenstein to have been the greatest master of public spectacle in the history of the cinema, and I am forgetting neither D. W. Griffith nor Cecil B. De Mille. He was a superb exponent of that tradition of collective art which is represented by the pageants of ancient Egypt, by the circuses in Rome, by the ritual of the Roman Catholic Church, and by all the many and varied collective manifestations of faith. That he has come to reflect novelties in film technique is less important for me than his membership of an ancient theatrical tradition that was shortly to be found once again in the work of Leni Riefenstahl, or the Duke of Norfolk's presentation of the Coronation, or in the colossal resources of the Army, Navy, and Air Force at the funeral of Sir Winston Churchill. It was Eisenstein who could attack the Winter Palace with the citizens of Leningrad, and in *Battleship Potemkin* could use the people of Odessa on their famous steps.

'This was at the very centre of his achievement, but he was also a man who reacted very directly to all the forces of his time, and especially to the great new world of industry and technology. In his art he sought to mirror the colossal power and resources of this world. He wanted the cinema, by its use of movement, to reflect the great industrial masses of the age, to turn the film into what he called a "demonstration of mass man". To some extent he achieved this in his own work at the expense of human relationships, and a fault that I have more modestly shared with him is a lack of interest in people for their own sake. In Eisenstein's case he was much influenced by a phrase of his own master in the theatre, Meyerhold, who once referred to certain theatrical pieces as being about "worthless soul junk", and they were both trying to flee from this "junk" into what they saw as a much bigger world where simple statements were made for the great masses of the people. Eisenstein proceeded to do this, not only in terms of the army, the navy and the citizenry, but by using imaginatively the most colossal resource ever to be made available to the cinema, which is Industry itself. . . .

'. . . I have never been fond of intellectual theorizing, and we all know how a philosophy can be the product of necessity. We know that the main reason why Eisenstein developed his first Soviet films in movements, like a symphony, was that in nearly every Russian cinema in those days there was only one projector, and the reels had to be changed every ten or twelve minutes. We ourselves had the same problem when we began to build up "non-theatrical" distribution in Britain. We felt that the existence of a single projector justified our approach to the film in terms of a series of "movements", and later there were schools of students who wrote in learned journals to say how aesthetically brilliant we were.'

Taken as a whole *October* is less disciplined than *Battleship Potemkin* and suffers from some of the defects of *Strike*, mixing satire with realism and naturalism with fantasy. Many of its most brilliant passages are more splendid in isolation than as integral parts of a complete film. The sequence of Kerensky climbing the apparently endless steps of the Winter Palace – the real steps, for the Palace was Eisenstein's location – and plodding his way to the height of pseudo-Tsarist power is a fine piece of political satire, but it is stylistically the absolute opposite of the attack on the Palace itself, or the totally realistic scene at the Finland Station when Lenin addresses the crowd on his return from exile in April 1917. The attack on the Palace is a reconstruction of an actual event, but the sequence in which the statue of the Tsar falls to the ground in pieces, its head, arms, and crown falling not once each but over and over again, is an imaginative image of the fall of an Imperial dynasty, but is of course nonsense in every documentary sense.

Unlike *Strike* and *Battleship Potemkin*, *October* is a film that had to give reasonable prominence to known historical figures, and in this area also Eisenstein was deliberately inconsistent. Lenin, played by a non-actor, V. Nikandrov, is treated with little imagination and no inventive-

Eisenstein seated on the Tsar's throne in the Winter Palace

ness whatever, so that he is rarely more than the conventional figure of the posters and socialist-realist paintings. Yet Kerensky, played by a student (N. Popov) who bore a striking resemblance to the man himself, is presented as a figure of farce, arousing neither anger nor pity but loud laughter, much as Chaplin – who might well have been influenced by the work of his Russian friend – treated his Great Dictator.

Both *October* and *The Great Dictator* are political films, but Eisenstein's was also a party and a patriotic film, designed to glorify the Bolsheviks and to be a mammoth celebration of a revolution which had

October. V. Nikandrov as Lenin addresses the crowd at the Finland Station

his own full support. For him it could never have been just a 'job of work' – a phrase that can hardly be used of anything he ever did, except for two very minor chores in France and Switzerland – but a dedicated piece of art in support of a form of society that he respected and admired, and which in its turn had shown its appreciation of his own talents by the commissions it gave him. It is important to remember this in considering Eisenstein's work both before and after his journey to the West, and in assessing the value of his numerous written

October. Some of the film-makers with some of the cast in the Winter Palace. Eisenstein seated in the centre. Below him, to the left, is Tisse, and to the right Alexandrov

volumes devoted to the theory of film. The point has been well made by Jay Leyda, a friend and student of Eisenstein:

'Eisenstein has discussed in detail certain means whereby the spectator's reactions can be fused with the creative process, producing a richer emotional expression of a film's theme. But the thoroughness with which he investigates these means should mislead no one into assuming that in his view they represent ends in themselves, or that an emotion or a sensation represents an end in itself. The purposive direction of the spectator's emotion is a social responsibility, and all art in the Soviet Union is conscious of that responsibility in times of peace as well as war. This social function . . . underlines every word of Eisenstein's film theory.'[3]

This ultimate purpose also controlled Eisenstein's work both with the camera and in the cutting-room, and was the *'raison d'être'* of his 'montage of attractions' in the cinema as well as in the theatre. It was arguably his main contribution to the silent film, and most certainly it was the aspect of his early work that differed most profoundly from that of his contemporaries in other countries. He did not, for example, 'invent' the close-up or the dramatic value of inter-cutting, and of course the word 'montage' is neither Russian nor English. He freely admitted his debt to D. W. Griffith, and especially to *Intolerance*, and he followed the work of the film-makers of Berlin: Lang, Murnau, Lubitsch, and Wiene. He was also familiar with the rising French cinema of Clair, Feyder, Gance, and Renoir.

An advantage of being a film-maker in the Soviet Union has always been that of financial support and the positive encouragement of all ideas which are not regarded as politically 'mistaken'. So Eisenstein was indisputably happy in the 1920s, and seems quietly to have accepted political 'advice' during the editing of *October*. If he complained, then few of his complaints, other than an occasional moan about technical facilities in Leningrad, have been recorded. Alexandrov's attitude is that in 1927, at the peak of the Trotskyite dispute, some degree of political interference was a fact of life.

October, like *Strike*, had weaknesses of which Eisenstein was himself well aware. In November 1927, when he was still working on it in the cutting-room, he was visited by the French critic, Léon Moussinac, who later described Eisenstein's feelings about *October* at that time:

'Eisenstein himself was aware that side by side with the overpowering sequences . . . there were other sequences of considerably lesser quality, and he foresaw that this film could never be "complete" in the way he would have liked. He knew perfectly well that it would have to undergo certain revisions and cuts, and that even under the best of circumstances only fragments would be shown abroad. . . .'[4]

In a letter to Moussinac, written in December 1928, Eisenstein wrote:

'From the point of view of construction, *October* is by no means flawless. It is just that in this film that is so much of "the people", of the "masses", I allowed myself to experiment. Despite the fact that my experiments are seldom appreciated . . . they were enough to break the composition of the work as a unity. But on the other hand they were also enough to allow me to make deductions which are very, very far-reaching.'[5]

It was perhaps unwise of Eisenstein to 'allow' himself to 'experiment' with a film whose subject-matter was as sensitive as that of the October Revolution, and its reception in the Soviet Union was by no means either unanimous or enthusiastic. The film historian Nikolai Lebedev, looking back in 1947, confirmed this by dismissing it as one of the 'conspicuous failures of the experimental cinema' (adding that Eisenstein's next film *Old and New* was another), and went on to make this comment: 'Eisenstein considered that the basic facts of the October days were generally known, so that he presented not these but, by his own admission, "my own associations, my visual puns", that those facts called to mind.'[6] It is also true that of all the films made in celebration of the tenth anniversary of the October Revolution, Eisenstein's was the last to be shown. The audience which applauded *The End of St Petersburg*, by his rival Pudovkin, at the Bolshoi Theatre on the precise day of the anniversary, had to wait another four months for the chance to see the complete version of *October*. In the meantime numerous changes were made in the cutting-room, and there were strong rumours in the world's press that both Eisenstein and Alexandrov were supporters of Trotsky, and suffered accordingly. The rumours were absurd, and Eisenstein publicly denied them.

Eisenstein's next finished film was to be his last Soviet 'silent' film, and also his last work to be completed for nearly ten years. Work on *Old and New* had in fact begun before he was asked to make *October*, and was resumed in the early summer of 1928. Another political film, its theme is the rural revolution brought to Russian agriculture by collectivization, and the introduction of modern methods of farming, but this time the film has a particular human 'heroine'. Marfa Lapkina, a peasant woman, protests against the general ignorance and apathy of

Eisenstein during the shooting of *Old and New*, 1929

her own district, and with the help of the official representatives of the new policy she inspires her neighbours to form a co-operative. Eisenstein used a cream-separator as the symbol of the new mechanical age, and one of the most moving scenes in the film is when the local people stand round this startling piece of equipment, waiting with varying degrees of hope and scepticism for the first drops of cream. Will it work or are they being deceived? To suggest this doubt in visual terms Eisenstein daringly inserted into the sequence the recurring image of a roulette wheel. Inevitably the cream appears and as the first drops become larger and larger until the whole world seems about to be drowned in the thick white liquid, Eisenstein intercuts the machine and

Marfa Lapkina, the real-life heroine of *Old and New*

its cream with the faces of the peasants – all of them non-actors – as their reactions change from scepticism to absolute joy. It is one of the most lyrical passages in the whole of Eisenstein's work, totally successful both as propaganda and as a human poem.

Technical progress and the 'new' form of agricultural organization are the answers given in *Old and New* to those whose faith lies in religious superstition. The sequence of the cream-separator is in sharp contrast, both visually and in the tempo of its editing, to the equally famous sequence when the villagers, in time of drought, march in pilgrimage to pray for rain. Their prayers are not answered, but the modern machine and the social enthusiasm of men and women together succeed. This vain pilgrimage, people and priests kneeling together on

Old and New. Eisenstein with some of the technical team, including Tisse, seated on the right

the parched earth and gazing helplessly at the bare sky and the blazing sun, is another sequence both moving and human. The two sequences together seem to suggest that in *Old and New* Eisenstein had realized that if the mass audience is to be fully persuaded then it must never be confused.

In *Old and New* Alexandrov is again credited as both co-director and co-author of the script, and once more both Strauch and Gomorov were Eisenstein's assistants. Eduard Tisse was the cameraman, and so the credits for Eisenstein's first four films include many of the same names, and most of these had worked with him at the old Proletkult Theatre. Maxim Strauch looked back from a distance of forty years at his experience with Eisenstein in the cinema of the 1920s, and summed it up in this way:

'I was one of five actors who left the theatre with Eisenstein in 1924, sharing his enthusiasm for the new medium of the cinema and accepting what was for all of us both a search and an experiment; the others were Alexandrov, Gomorov, Levshin, and Antonov, and we became widely known as "The Iron Five" – the phrase was coined by a newspaper reporter who saw us working together and was obviously impressed by our image of corporate toughness. We walked about in striped football shorts, looking like a pack of zebras, which was Eisenstein's way of making sure that we were conspicuous enough to be easily located in a crowd scene.

'He liked to take big historical events as a whole, like a pageant, accepting them as total occasions and reflecting as best he could their immense size. This size was for him a barometer of their importance, and this is why his films are so densely populated. Each "character" makes a very brief appearance, often for a few seconds only, like a mother carrying a dead boy on the Odessa Steps, the wounded woman with the perambulator, the schoolmistress with the broken glasses. They are on the screen for only a few feet at a time, but together they contribute totally to the full impact of the entire sequence. So for Eisenstein what we would nowadays call "type-casting" was of basic importance. Each "type" had to present his credentials in a single frame, and so he had to be much more that just a "personality". He had to be a whole way of life.

'This "type-casting" was a process in which I found myself more frequently involved than the other "Iron Men", though we all took part in it from time to time. Eisenstein would issue his orders for the man-hunt, and like vultures we set off to scour the city or the country-side for our prey. For the famous sequence in *Old and New* in which the villagers march in procession praying for rain, we chose our victims during a night-long search of Leningrad's doss-houses. The peasant-heroine of the same film, Marfa Lapkina, was herself a farm-worker who could neither read nor write, and she was found at the last minute, when we were almost in despair. The man who played Lenin in

October. Some of the people of Leningrad as they appeared in the film

October was a factory worker with no previous experience of acting, and whose only qualifications were those of a striking physical resemblance. His part was of course a principal one, and so was that of Marfa Lapkina, but each face that appeared on the screen, whether alone or as part of a crowd, had its individual importance, and I myself spent dozens of days and nights searching the streets and offices, doss-houses and bars, often disguising myself by assuming the dress and the manner of the people I was looking for. To find the right person was not, of course, the end of our problem. There was the job of persuading the victim to take part, to get a husband's permission for the filming of his wife, to get a man to shave off a moustache that he had worn for the best part of his life. Sometimes it was even necessary to prove that an appearance on the screen is not really a sin in the eyes of God. Usually we succeeded, for the chance to take part in a film has always been a temptation too powerful for most people to resist.'[7]

The Moscow première of *Old and New* took place on the twelfth anniversary of the Revolution – 7 November 1929 – but for once Eisenstein was not present, and neither were Alexandrov nor Tisse. They had already left for Berlin on a journey that was to take them to Western Europe, the USA and Mexico, and they were to be away from their country for two and a half years. The reason for the trip was to study the use of synchronized sound, which at that time had not yet been developed in the Soviet cinema. But such a journey presented problems that were more than just technical; they were also political and philosophical, and Eisenstein himself was well aware of them:

'To go abroad – it presents the ultimate test that one can set a Soviet citizen whose life has been inseparable from the October Revolution: the test of a free choice. Going abroad offers the final challenge to the creative worker: to prove whether he can really create outside the Revolution; whether he can even exist outside it.'

3

The Western Experiment

On 4 June 1929 Eisenstein had written from Moscow to Léon Moussinac, outlining his immediate plans and ambitions. 'My personal
future', he wrote, 'is gradually taking shape. It is my obsession to add
sound to *Old and New*, and to do that I must go abroad. . . . Then, after
the European première I want to go to the United States. The Hollywood side of the USA doesn't interest me at all; I want to see the
country! And the techniques of sound films. For I am absolutely
certain that the entire future of the cinema lies with sound.'[1] Granted
that belief, the United States was the obvious place to visit.

He left Moscow with Alexandrov and Tisse in the middle of August
and attended the German première of *Old and New* in Berlin. From
there they proceeded to the château of La Sarraz, near Lausanne in
Switzerland, where the châtelaine, Mme de la Mandrot, had heroi-
cally offered her house as a meeting-place for a group of avant-garde
film-makers. It was a conference that included among its sponsors
André Gide, Pirandello, and Stefan Zweig, and among those who
attended were Walther Ruttman from Berlin, the Italian futurist
Enrico Prampolini, Jean-George Auriol who edited *Revue du Cinéma*,
Alberto Cavalcanti, Montgomery Evans from the USA, Hiroshi Hijo
from Japan, Léon Moussinac and the critic Janine Bouissonouse from
Paris, the surrealist Hans Richter, and from London Ivor Montagu
and Jack Isaacs. The three Russians had eagerly accepted an invitation
to attend the conference, and their impact on this somewhat élitist
and self-conscious gathering has been described by Ivor Montagu:
'Before they arrived we had all been sitting and chatting together in

this gorgeous "château", with its superb tapestry and its medieval walls, admiring each other's films and saying how wonderful and imaginative and important was everything we had done. Then, suddenly and as though from outer space, there came these three characters from the Soviet Union. As far as we were concerned they were already magnificent before they spoke a single word or performed a single action. We all knew and admired *Battleship Potemkin*, and we regarded Eisenstein as an almost divine figure. And now here they were, three men in boiler suits; Eisenstein himself was short and squat, with the huge head that we already recognized from photographs,

La Sarraz, 1929. Delegates to the International Film Conference. Alexandrov is seated on the lowest step on the left; Eisenstein is second from the right on the second step; Ivor Montagu is seated on the extreme left on the third step

and a gigantic quiff, and eyes that sparkled with an amiable malice. The other two, Alexandrov and Tisse, were extremely good-looking, one younger than the other, but each with golden hair and golden skin, and both of them full of boundless energy.

'For three or four hours our Soviet visitors behaved impeccably; and then they suggested that we should all stop talking and make a film. The immediate consequence of this proposal – which of course the rest of us accepted at once – was total annihilation of poor Mme de la Mandrot. Her precious shields, the costumes and helmets and rare old weapons . . . everything was dragged from the walls. We were then all enlisted by Eisenstein and his two friends into a film that was really a dramatic "simile" of the commercial cinema, in which the art of film was at first imprisoned and then rescued by the assembled intellectuals of La Sarraz. We all wore costumes of various shapes and colours and periods of history, but Eisenstein was careful not to make himself the director. He just ran about as a general dog's-body. It was my first introduction to him, and what I remember from it most of all are his boyish spirits.'

No doubt Eisenstein enjoyed the effusive hero-worship of La Sarraz, but it failed to provide him with one of the basic necessities of life: it earned him no money. The three Russians had left Moscow with exactly twenty-five dollars each, and the only ways of sustaining themselves in the West were the charity of their friends or the commissions of film companies. Charity let them live as heroes at La Sarraz, but it was the need to earn a professional living that took them from there to Zürich, where a young Swiss producer, Lazar Wechsler, had suggested to Eisenstein that he might direct a documentary on the subject of abortion. The offer was accepted; but Eisenstein soon left for Berlin, and the credits on the completed film – improbably called *Woman's Joy is Woman's Woe* – name Eduard Tisse as its director. One sequence was the personal work of Eisenstein* and it portrays a slum family expecting yet another child; the mother has an illegal abortion and

---

* What I have written is based upon personal conversations with Grigori Alexandrov and Lazar Wechsler. Yet there is internal evidence to suggest that Eisenstein was only in Zürich for one day—hardly long enough for him to direct a complete sequence.

suffers serious physical damage as a result of the incompetence of the doctor who performs it.

While Tisse pursued abortion in Zürich, Eisenstein enjoyed himself in Berlin, studying its bizarre night-life, arguing with its film-makers, being lionized by its intellectuals, and generally cultivating the society of the successful and the fashionable. Always a man who picked up 'names' as frequently as others drop them, he was seen in the company of Berthold Brecht, Ernst Toller, Fritz Lang, Pabst, Pirandello, and Albert Einstein. Then in November 1929 he collected his two friends in Zürich and together they all went to Paris where the editing of *Woman's Joy is Woman's Woe* was completed.

In Paris Eisenstein continued to explore the great and the famous, enjoying the stimulus of their company and testing his own wisdom against theirs. He met Cocteau and Léger, and he received a first edition of *Ulysses* signed by its author. René Clair described him as 'a smiling lion, loaded with hair, and always laughing'. At the invitation of Léon Moussinac he lectured at the Sorbonne, where at the last minute he was prevented by the French police from showing a few selected sequences from *Old and New*. He visited the Louvre, Nôtre-Dame, and the flea-market, and he roamed the streets of the city and enjoyed its fashionable cafés. He also toured France with Moussinac and his wife.

It would be unfair to imply that his interest in human beings was limited to those who were successful and famous. He had an equal concern for those who were young, talented, and still struggling for recognition, and inevitably they still remember him with a lasting affection. One of them, living in Paris in 1929, was the Dutch film-maker Joris Ivens, who several years later was to join Ernest Hemingway in Spain and make the most famous of all the documentaries to be inspired by the Civil War – *Spanish Earth*. His recollection of Eisenstein in 1929 is typical of those who were young and enthusiastic.

'I often find it hard to remember exactly when I first met my closest friends, and in the case of Eisenstein I suspect that our first meeting was at a time when I had never yet been introduced to him in the physical sense at all. I believe that our first true meeting was when I saw *Battleship Potemkin* and I remember that he once returned the compliment by telling me that our first meeting was when he saw my own very modest beginning as a film-maker: a little documentary called *Rain*. The truth is that *Battleship Potemkin* had the same effect on me as it had on every young film-maker at that time. It was an experience both immediate and unforgettable. Moreover – and this is too often forgotten or ignored – it was the work of a young man of twenty-seven. He and I were born in the same year, and so I must have been in my own twenties when I first saw it. So my first "meeting" with Eisenstein was no more and no less than the shattering impact on a young novice of a work of genius by a young master. The subject-matter of the film was revolution, a small corner of the abortive Russian revolution of 1905, but for me what has always been much more important is that it was itself a complete revolution in the history of that seventh art, the cinema.

'Battleship Potemkin* is both more and less than fiction, both more and less than documentary, an indictment of the familiar cliché that a film must be either a "feature" (i.e. fiction), or a "documentary" (i.e. the creative reflection of fact). Such facile definitions collapse altogether in the face of a masterpiece, for "masterpiece" is how most of us described *Battleship Potemkin* in the 1920s and how I myself would still describe it. But in those faraway days the practical problem was how and where to show it, for a film made in the Soviet Union, and a film moreover which had revolution as its theme, was a highly dangerous property. It was too easy for the authorities to condemn it as "propaganda", and for many people in positions of power in Western Europe it carried all the menace of a secret weapon. In several countries – in France and Britain for instance – it was denied a general public showing for many years, and those of us who felt it to be a great and significant work of art found ourselves engaged in a fierce political battle on its behalf, arranging private screenings, and trying to break down blatant examples of censorship.

'I am writing all this in order to explain my sense of having known Eisenstein before I met him. Then, in 1929, the creator of *Battleship Potemkin* came to Paris, and I saw him for the first time, face to face. How would I describe him? Firstly as a man who combined that rare duet of virtues – lucidity and intelligence. Then as someone who had not only read more than any man I had ever met, but who could also recall with absolute precision any quotation from any of the books known to him. Whenever I quoted to him from Shakespeare, or Stendhal, or Tolstoy, or from a contemporary writer like James Joyce, he would not only say, "Ah yes, that comes from this book or that book," but he could repeat from memory, accurately and in the original language, whatever piece I chanced to mention. Nor was his talent in this direction limited to literature. He could remember every shot of every film that he and I had ever seen, and if I referred to a painting by El Greco or van Gogh or any other major artist, he could describe it with precise accuracy, exactly as it was.

'Many of his friends have written about his famous sense of humour, which indeed was one of the most conspicuous aspects of his personality, and it went with him everywhere. Often, when we walked together in Paris, he would take his camera with him, but the subjects he chose to photograph were never the conventional "sights" of the city, but human beings in comical situations. I suspect that this highly developed and very conspicuous sense of fun might have been a form of compensation for his basic shyness. For although he was undoubtedly a very good friend to many people in many countries, he was far less emotional in his personal friendships than most others I have known. With Eisenstein, and especially at the beginning of a relationship, there was a feeling of reserve. He must have been conscious of this, and might even have been ashamed of it, trying to compensate for it by an excessively extroverted sense of humour.'

In Paris, as earlier in Switzerland, the three Russians could only survive by earning much more money than was likely to be provided either by their personal friends or by lectures at the Sorbonne, and this time it was Alexandrov who found the necessary opportunity. His charm persuaded a rich Parisian jeweller to sponsor a short film whose main purpose was to display the talents of his wife, a Russian singer named Mara Giry, who shared the leading roles with two vast white grand pianos. The film's title, by no means inappropriate, was *Romance Sentimentale*, and although Eisenstein's name appears on its credits as co-director, it was largely the work of Alexandrov. But it contains one sequence that bears the unmistakable signature of Eisenstein himself, an opening montage of Nature, trees and water, of clouds and wind and rain, edited to a mixed track of music and natural sounds. He had

come to the West with the expressed purpose of studying the technique
of the sound film, and it was Alexandrov's French jeweller who gave
him this first opportunity to experiment with some of the ways in
which images and sounds might be used together both creatively and
emotively. Eisenstein himself later wrote a fair summary of *Romance
Sentimentale* in a letter to Léon Moussinac: 'You know very well that
there's not a lot of me in it (to say the least), except for the principles
and possibilities of sound utilization that are popularized in it. . . . In
any case we got what we wanted from it; we made some *very valuable*
montage experiments, and it gave us enough money to stay in Paris.'[2]

At La Sarraz Eisenstein had been invited by Ivor Montagu and Jack
Isaacs to visit London as the guest of the Film Society, to give a series
of lectures and to attend the British première of *Battleship Potemkin*. He
had accepted the invitation, and now he found time to leave Paris for
a brief stay in Britain.

The London Film Society, which on Sunday afternoons presented
programmes of films that for one reason or another were unlikely to
receive wide public distribution, now offered its members a historic
'double bill', consisting of John Grierson's *Drifters* and Eisenstein's
Battleship Potemkin. It was an occasion more appreciated by the young
cinéastes of London than the Russian whose work they had come to
worship; never a man to enjoy the stealing of his own thunder – even
by a supremely talented Scot – he pretended that *Drifters* had given
away some of the best parts of *Battleship Potemkin* and made a joke of
the fact that the Film Society's version of his own picture was shown
to a musical score by the German Edmund Meisel which transformed
a fine film into a 'mediocre opera'. His lectures, which pleased him
more, were presented as part of a course of film studies that also included a lesson in practical film-making under the direction of another
of the men of La Sarraz, Hans Richter. The course was inconclusive,
and the film was never finished. All that remains is a brief sequence in
which Eisenstein mimes the part of a London policeman. It is typical
of his sense of satirical observation and, also typically, was never in the
original script.

On the other hand, his lectures, delivered in excellent English, were a complete success. In London, as at the school of cinematography in Moscow, he startled his students by insisting that film was not in itself a pure art form but a synthesis of many other and earlier arts made possible by the technology of the twentieth century. The young enthusiasts of London's Film Society were gripped by that obsessive enthusiasm which film, more readily than any other art, seems able to inspire in those who study it. For such young people Eisenstein's approach came as a salutary shock, and for those of them who were still humble enough to put aside their own youthful opinions his lectures were not only a signpost for a new direction of thought but a practical lesson that a few among his audience learnt to their lasting benefit. One of them, soon to become a major figure in British documentary, was Basil Wright:

'There we were, with notebooks and pencils, thinking passionately about film, the great new art form; and there was Eisenstein, chubbily built, plump in face; a pliable and expressive nose; a shock of dark hazel-coloured curly hair rising briskly above an imposing brow. There he was, with blackboard and chalk, about to expose us to the inner Eisenstein mysteries of film art.

'But what happened? He talked instead about Japanese Kabuki plays, about William James and Charles Darwin, Toulouse-Lautrec and Daumier; about Kenyon's proposition that "two opposite reactions can be provoked by the same stimulus"; about Duchenne's studies of muscular movements, and his conclusion that *"L'action musculaire isolé n'existe pas dans l'expression humaine"*; about Stefan Zweig, Zola, and James Joyce.

'As the lectures progressed we began to understand and appreciate all these surprising references. Eisenstein never forgot that film is a synthetic art. He made it clear that for him the approach to film theory, and in particular to montage, was not something in a vacuum. He claimed, in fact, that film montage was the *cinematic* aspect of a particular form of expression used by artists in other media – and particularly in poetry, painting, drama, and the novel. Let me quote from my own notes of his final lecture: "Only recently have we begun to feel the real type of filmic film which is to come. So far films moving in this direction have been purely experimental, but now the historical moment has come at which we are to find the synthesis of art and science in an entirely new form of picturization. This new form is not symbolic, but vital and *picturesque*. The method of expression is purely dynamic, like music; but not so impressionistic as music. In the new film sound will play a very large role, but the big developments will *not* come from the techniques of sound. Sound will in fact become one of the elements of the new montage system."

'Montage is a rather irritating word that has been much reviled in its day. It has been regarded as merely a synonym for editing and cutting, but it is quite clear that Eisenstein meant much more than that. It does of course imply fundamentally that the editing process is a key to good film-making, but it also implies that the whole aesthetic conception of film shape, film structure, filmic expression, resides in the fact that film is synthetic. Synthesis – the putting together of material in such a way that the sum of the various units produces an entirely new quality, an unknown "X".

'One of the things that Eisenstein said in his first lecture was this: "Go the way the material calls you; the scenario changes on location, and the location shots change in the montage". So for me, at any rate, Eisenstein's lectures pointed clearly towards what I call the *instinctive* approach to film-making, in opposition to the commoner conception of *controlled* production – more common in 1929 than today – with cast-iron scripts and elaborate schedules. From Eisenstein I learnt to be suspicious of a shooting-script. On location, as in the cutting-room, his analysis of film theory meant for me the making of a film *to an idea* rather than, as was normal, to a previously constructed and highly logical story-continuity. This obviously implies working in a rather different field from the studio conception of story-telling, but it by no means implies confusion or extravagance. Nor does it prevent the telling of a story.'[3]

The young Basil Wright was also in the audience when *Drifters* and *Battleship Potemkin* were shown together, and the combination of those two events – the screening of the films and Eisenstein's lectures – 'made it inevitable that I should try to get a job with Grierson'. It was this direct link between Eisenstein's brief visit to London and the British documentary movement of the 1930s which arguably made it the most significant part of his journey to the West. In Berlin, Switzerland, and Paris the only lasting effect of his visit had been the opening sequence of *Romance Sentimentale*. In Hollywood he would create nothing and would leave in despair; and the magnificent material to be shot in Mexico was still in other hands at the time of his death. But in London, by one of those chances which by their timing have produced new and profound developments in all the arts, Eisenstein's lectures and the first British screening of *Battleship Potemkin* coincided with the early childhood of the most creative documentary movement in the history of the cinema.

John Grierson, the accepted 'father' of the movement and the maker of *Drifters*, had already worked on the American version of *Battleship Potemkin* and he never hesitated to acknowledge his personal debt to Eisenstein:

'Someone, in forgetting the revolutionary pageantry in *Battleship Potemkin*, had remembered the battleship's thrilling engines. These engines at last came into their own, and the consequence was that little film called *Drifters*. Later, when we were in business ourselves, we became aware in a very practical way of Eisenstein's genius at film-editing. He was concerned with the impact of one image on another, and he expressed his attitude by arguing that "two particulars make a concept". Put one image together with another image, and you get an idea. Eisenstein, moreover, used his images to create an explosive impact on the physical self of the spectator rather than merely to produce a linkage in narrative.

'He also knew, though he spoke of it less frequently, that when you put two images together you can create much more than a "concept": you can create poetry. For me the most moving scene in all Eisenstein's work is the sequence in *Old and New* where the peasant woman, Marfa (surely the most beautiful face in film history), gets a milk separator to work. In that marvellous passage Eisenstein used the art of montage, and the assembling of images, to express untold joy, and this achievement is pure poetry.

'All of us in the British documentary were influenced by Eisenstein's "montage", but in its poetic possibilities rather than its intellectual ambition. For myself, for example, I made a mast and I made a bird fly over the mast, and the mast seemed higher and more lonely because of the bird flying over it. If you want to know where the courage of poetry in *Song of Ceylon* came from, or the courage of poetry in *Night Mail*, then you must go to the poetic rather than the violent sequences of Eisenstein.'

When Basil Wright made *Song of Ceylon* he was very much under the influence of both Eisenstein's films and his London lectures:

'In Ceylon, instead of filming to a planned, pre-conceived script, and to a definite story-continuity, I was working, through Eisenstein's conception of montage, to shoot everything to a central idea. By this I mean that all the filmic material – the many strips of celluloid depicting different scenes – was related to a central conception which in its turn was no more and no less than a deep *feeling* about this particular island. I was unable then, as I am now, to express this feeling in words. It belongs strictly to the flow and movement of visuals, and could only be expressed in that manner.

'Surely it was because of this montage conception during the shooting that the material came miraculously together on the cutting-bench. The flank of an elephant, in big close-up, passing the camera, juxtaposed itself with a close-up of the sail of a passing outrigger boat, and I've often noted with interest how this particular bit of montage has affected viewers emotionally. Similarly, shots of birds flying across the rippling waters of a lake interwove themselves with rapid panning shots of the grave, serene faces of granite Buddhas; faces which at that stage were only glimpsed, but were reintroduced as dominating motives in a later sequence.

'I also attempted a parallel technique with the film's sound track, and if *Song of Ceylon* has any merits then much of the credit must go to that first clear formulation of film theory put forward by Eisenstein during those lectures in London in 1929.'[4]

So Eisenstein's short visit to Britain gave practical evidence of his genius as a teacher, which was to reach its peak several years later in his own country. Indeed on every level the visit was an undisputed success. His lectures were influential, *Battleship Potemkin* became for those who saw it a huge landmark in film history, and personally he charmed and impressed everyone he met. For Jack Isaacs he remained 'the most intelligent man I ever knew, and one of the nicest, with a sense of humour both robust and Rabelaisian'. Basil Wright, like many others before and after, was reminded of a twentieth-century Leonardo da Vinci, and Herbert Marshall, later to become his student in Moscow, behaved with such deference that Eisenstein himself said plaintively to Ivor Montagu that he was 'so very worshipping'.

In May 1930, nearly nine months after leaving Moscow, Eisenstein arrived in the United States. That at last he received an invitation to work in Hollywood was largely due to the diplomacy of Ivor Montagu, who had gone there ahead of him to work on his own and had used his contacts with Paramount to achieve what had seemed increasingly unlikely. The result of Montagu's good offices was that when Jesse L. Lasky, one of the heads of Paramount, visited Paris early in 1930 he contacted Eisenstein and approved the general terms of an agreement whose broad conditions were spelt out in an article that Eisenstein sent to Léon Moussinac for publication:

'After a movie at Paramount – to be completed in about six months – our team will return to Moscow for our next Soviet production. After that we shall return to Hollywood for a second film. We foresee a third and a fourth film under the same conditions, our team travelling to and fro between the USSR and America. If during the first three months of our stay in the USA we are unable to agree on a subject for the movie, or on working conditions, our relationship can be terminated, in which case we will return at once to Moscow.'

That version of the contract reads more optimistically than the account given by Ivor Montagu, whose recollection is that the arrangement was not so much 'a contract of service' as 'an agreement of Paramount to allow expenses for a period of six months'. Those expenses, granted the riches of Hollywood, seem surprisingly small: five hundred dollars for Eisenstein, and a hundred each for Alexandrov, Tisse, Montagu, and Montagu's wife. The assumption was that an increase in payment would follow the acceptance of a script; either that, or a firm farewell if no such agreement took place.

By the time the Russians reached Hollywood Montagu had rented a house for the entire team in Cold Water Canyon, which was where they lived and worked together on the scripts. Of all those who knew Eisenstein and his two colleagues in Hollywood, Ivor Montagu is by far the best qualified to write with authority:

'When anybody first arrives in Hollywood he is automatically the white-headed boy. Everything is laid out for him, and he is told, "Don't hurry, just take your time, sit down, absorb everything, enjoy the fleshpots, be entertained, meet all these wonderful people." So it was, at any rate, in the days of the great stars, and so it was for Eisenstein. We made a great many friends, and luckily I had already got to know Charlie Chaplin. It was Chaplin who became our great mainstay; we were constantly his guests, and his warm friendship was a tremendous relief from all the arduous struggles that came our way.

'We took a long time to settle on a subject. At first Eisenstein had the fantastic idea of making a picture about a "Glass House", a building made entirely of glass, and in which hundreds of people would be living and working. The point of the story was that these people, despite the glass walls, had no idea that they could all see each other until for some reason – such as the sudden arrival of a burglar – their suspicions were aroused and they immediately became aware of one another. The consequence was violent conflict. This vague theme needed a detailed plot but nobody, either from our own little group or from the team of writers at Paramount, proved capable of inventing one. But Eisenstein, instead of dropping the subject, started a course of psychoanalysis to discover why he himself couldn't think of anything else. And in the meantime we bathed, played tennis, saw the sights, and made more friends.'

In those days Hollywood, or indeed the entire west coast of the United States, was not exactly distinguished for intellectual achievement. Most of the novelists, painters, dramatists, poets and philosophers lived and flourished elsewhere, and whenever they were called to Hollywood they chose to work quickly, receive as much money as

possible, and go home. Eisenstein, who could never flourish in a
cultural desert, had already found time to lecture at Harvard, Col-
umbia, and Chicago, and spent a few days in Boston with H. W. L.
Dana, the grandson of the poet Longfellow. In Hollywood such delights
were harder to find, and he wrote to Moussinac that "on the intellectual level Hollywood is in the same class as Soissons or Brive", and with
few exceptions he found "everyone stupid or of mediocre interest".
He was photographed with Walt Disney – whose work, and especially
its use of sound, he much admired – Marlene Dietrich, Josef von

Hollywood, 1930. Eisenstein with Josef von Sternberg and Marlene
Dietrich

Sternberg, and Rin-Tin-Tin. Chaplin was one of those exceptions to his sad generalization; so were King Vidor, von Stroheim, Greta Garbo, Berthold Viertel and his wife Salka, and Lewis Milestone.

King Vidor, himself one of the finer products of Hollywood's golden days, has in his turn put on record his own recollections of the man from Moscow.

'The reason why I met Eisenstein in the first place was that he'd seen my latest film, *The Crowd*, in New York, and was intrigued by some of the technical devices used in it. For, after all, the professional reason for that long and devious journey from Moscow to Hollywood had been to study our latest production techniques. So I was happy to show him round the MGM studios, and several of the location sites as well. I remember his particular interest in what I can best describe as the first use of the "zoom", though it was really nothing of the kind, but a camera that could move forward and descend at the same time. He was also intrigued by another device we were using, which allowed us to take travelling shots up the side of a tall building. It was very soon clear to me that he and I, despite our national and political differences, really spoke the same language.

'Let me expand that last sentence by a story. There was an evening when he came to dinner, along with "Grisha" Alexandrov and Eduard Tisse, and after the meal we ran his last Russian film, *Old and New*. Our projectionist for the occasion was Tisse himself, and he got along fine until around the third or fourth reel; at which point Eisenstein jumped up, went to the booth, and told him that he'd put on the wrong reel. Tisse quietly assured him that he'd done nothing of the kind, and that the reel was undoubtedly the correct one. So they stopped the film altogether, came back into the room, and began to argue about whether it was the right reel or the wrong one. So here was one of the greatest film directors in the world, disagreeing with one of the finest cameramen the cinema has ever known, about the order of reels in a film they had both made together. I can no longer remember which of them was right. Maybe neither of them was.

'I believe that story to have an important moral for film directors. It proves that the film has its own form, and that this form is so dynamic that it has no need of a First Act, a Second Act, or a Third

Act. You don't have to follow the traditional forms of the theatre or the novel, because the form you are working in is an art form in its own right. Which is why Eisenstein could argue in all seriousness about the correct reel being on or not being on. In a play, or at any rate in the conventional plays of the 1930s, you soon got lost if you skipped from Scene Two to Scene Five. You also knew it soon enough if you began a novel with Chapter Six and then went back to Chapter One. But the film is different; which is what I meant when I used that phrase "the same language".

'Eisenstein and I used that same language when we spoke together about the power of certain scenes. I told him that although a particular film I once made was by this time almost entirely forgotten, I kept meeting people who remembered just one of its sequences. "Remember that scene?" they'd say, and then add "Now what film was it in, and who was in it?" All they could literally remember was the beauty, or the rhythm, of a particular sequence. This was an experience, and with it went a belief, that Eisenstein and I shared together; a faith in the unique and dynamic power of the camera and the cutting-room. Look at *Battleship Potemkin* today, study the design on the steps of Odessa, and the patterns of the people lying on the steps. To make a film you don't need actors moving about, speaking lines, and surviving familiar situations, and Eisenstein knew this better than most of us. He had the true vision of the motion-picture as its own medium of expression, and one which could draw on other art forms without blindly following their general direction. Eisenstein knew very well that in its own way the cinema was making art history just as the discovery of perspective had made art history in its own time.'

No doubt; but Eisenstein was in Hollywood, where few directors were as adventurous, or as persuasive with their employers, as King Vidor. There was that agreement with Paramount, and nothing to show for it so far except a vague idea about a house of glass that had inspired nobody at all. Let Ivor Montagu continue the sorry story:

'At long last we got down to work on a subject for a scenario. It was an idea that Eisenstein had brought with him from Europe, a novel in French by Blaise Cendrars and called *L'Or* or, in the English translation, *Sutter's Gold*. Its theme, which was founded on historical fact, was about the discovery of gold in California, but more particularly it was about an individual Swiss who early in the nineteenth century had left his own country to start farming on the West coast of America. Later, gold was discovered on his land, but instead of making him rich it reduced him to poverty; for all those who worked for him at once rushed away and started digging for gold. This extraordinary tale, full of moral lessons, was turned by Eisenstein – with some help from the rest of us – into what I still regard as a marvellous script. We took it to Paramount, who simply pointed out to us that nobody in America was interested in history, and it was very old-fashioned of us to think otherwise. It would be as dull, so they politely explained, as if we tried to make a film about Henry VIII in England – and this, of course, was before the famous film of Alexander Korda and Charles Laughton, and forty years before the British television series that was to be such an enormous success in the United States.

'It was hard to take seriously such naive reasons for rejection, and I believe the true reason lay among the conflicts that undoubtedly

Hollywood, 1930. Eisenstein in pursuit of *Sutter's Gold*

existed within the Paramount company. Those who were jealous of the others who'd signed us up were trying to discredit the ones who supported us. There were so many reputations at stake, and so much of the in-fighting that constantly occurs in most large organizations. At any rate the immediate outcome was in effect an order; either we must make a film of Theodore Dreiser's novel *An American Tragedy* or we were out on our necks.

'Dreiser's book is of course a very different subject altogether. It makes rather stodgy reading, but it could certainly be described as an important book, and indeed arguably a great one. It shows how the American society of its day, with all the snobberies and feelings of distinction between rich and poor, can influence an impressionable young man, and eventually produce a situation in which he has either committed a murder or not; at least it seems on the surface that he has done so. Certainly he wanted to. Did he or did he not do it? But that question is not the real point of the book, which is that he was sent to the electric chair for a crime that was truly the crime of society, an "American tragedy" therefore, rather than his own individual tragedy.

'We embarked on the script with a sense of doom, knowing very well that a group of foreigners, led by a Soviet director with two Soviet associates, would never be permitted to make a film whose theme was essentially a criticism of American society. But when the script was presented to Paramount we were showered with compliments. "This is a most wonderful script," they told us, "and it's the finest thing we've ever had in the Studio. You must go to New York at once." The reason for that last remark was supposedly a recognition of the fact that *An American Tragedy* is set on the East coast, and so we had to go there in search of locations. We left at a few hours' notice, but the film was never made. Shortly after our arrival in New York we went into the office of Jesse L. Lasky, the man who had sought out Eisenstein in Paris and asked him to work for Paramount, and he simply said to us, "We're very sorry, but your contract is ended." '

The published text of the scenario of *An American Tragedy*, credited to 'S. M. Eisenstein, G. V. Alexandrov, and Ivor Montagu' and 'Based on the novel by Theodore Dreiser', is certainly faithful to Dreiser's social purpose, and read with the knowledge that Paramount

Hollywood. Eisenstein in the garden of Ivor Montagu's house with
G. V. Alexandrov

was being publicly attacked for harbouring 'a messenger from Hell, a dangerous foreign Jew come to poison America . . . a red dog . . . a sadist, a monster . . . (etc.)', might easily be taken as evidence that Lasky and his colleagues were seeking an excuse to escape from an embarrassing contract. Both Paramount and Eisenstein had been visited by the police, and for Eisenstein it was not the first time; there had been problems on the Swiss frontier and tougher ones with the Prefect of Police in Paris. There is certainly a case to be made, and many of Eisenstein's admirers have never hesitated to make it, that his failure in Hollywood was no more and no less than part of that long chain of political victimization which continued with the persecution of the 'Hollywood Ten' in the late 1940s, and the activities of Senator Joseph McCarthy's Un-American Activities Committee a few years later. Yet Ivor Montagu has always and significantly refused to accept this as more than a part of a very complex situation:

'Why did the enterprise fail? Some people have said the reasons were political, a basic fear of a Bolshevik who represented Bolshevism. This factor undoubtedly existed, and there were various elements of the lunatic fringe who ran around writing letters to the papers and making demonstrations about how Paramount had betrayed America by signing up this notorious Red Dog, and a great deal of angry correspondence arrived in the company's offices. All this must inevitably have carried some weight when it came to making the final decision, but to claim that this was the only reason for Eisenstein's failure in Hollywood is to make a great over-simplification. If this had been the only problem I doubt whether Paramount would have surrendered to it. I am sure that the bitter internal struggle within the company was just as responsible, the really fierce battle between those who supported us and those who tried to defeat them by proving how shameful we really were. Lastly, but of considerable importance, was the general fear that existed in Hollywood in those days – it is far less common in the cinema nowadays, thank goodness – of anybody with intellectual pretensions; and the brutal fact is that not only did we have intellectual pretensions, but we had them written all over us.'

This last point is echoed by King Vidor:

'Because Eisenstein knew he was handling a new art form, and because in personality he was the man he was, he refused in Hollywood to compromise his ideals or be talked out of the way he himself saw things. Anybody who behaved like that in California in the 1930s was bound to be heading for a pile of trouble, and in my view this is really why he failed. I would never deny the political reasons, and in my experience of him he was a deeply political animal – the man who when he ran my own film *Halleluyah* was more interested in the fact that it had an all-Negro cast than in any merits it might or might not have as a movie. Eisenstein was certainly a political animal, and a Soviet political animal moreover, but I honestly believe that he failed to get his scenarios accepted in Hollywood for reasons that simply add up to a failure of communication. Shakespeare wrote that the play's the thing; but in our own profession that is by no means necessarily true, and if the producing company had only recognized that fact, and had gone on from there to understand Eisenstein's personal vision, his true sense of what the cinema can do, then he might have succeeded. But the pattern in all our studios at that time was the conventional one of telling a story and going through the normal routine – the play's the thing – , and Eisenstein was already seeing far beyond that. They just failed to understand his approach, and he refused to compromise. Today we have men like Fellini and Antonioni, whose ideas would have been regarded as even more way-out than Eisenstein's in those days, but who are totally acceptable in the commercial cinema of the 1970s. The evolution of the film industry in the United States has long ago passed the point where Eisenstein's ideas could raise the eyebrows of the studio executives, and I have no doubt whatever that he would be allowed, for example, to make *Sutter's Gold* in Hollywood today. But of course Eisenstein was hardly the only artist in the history of the world to suffer by being ahead of his time.'

If Eisenstein and his colleagues had been willing to compromise, and had written a scenario for *An American Tragedy* which kept within the limits of what they must all have known to be acceptable, what then? Would Paramount have agreed to a conventional product, made to the familiar pattern outlined by King Vidor? There is at least one good reason for answering those questions in the affirmative; for shortly after Eisenstein had left Hollywood for ever a film version of

An American Tragedy was indeed produced there. The director was another European, Josef von Sternberg, and the production company was Paramount.

Yet the questions are academic. It was never in Eisenstein's nature to compromise in areas which concerned his artistic integrity, his political convictions, or his social conscience, and Dreiser's novel, and its adaptation for the screen, involved all those things very directly. Hence the sense of doom which the Russians and their associates experienced as soon as they were told that their future in Hollywood depended entirely on *An American Tragedy*. They knew perfectly well that they could only deliver a scenario that was faithful both to the letter and the spirit of the novel, and they also knew that such a scenario would be totally unacceptable in 1930.

Sutter's Gold was a different case. Although its theme was of a kind to appeal to a convinced socialist, its moral and social messages were indirect and oblique; and six years later it also was made into a Hollywood film (though not by Paramount). This suggests that Ivor Montagu's three reasons for the team's failure are the correct ones: an element of political victimization combined with internal rivalries within the company, and what King Vidor calls 'a failure of communication' between Eisenstein's personal vision and what Hollywood regarded as the only possible way to make a movie.

One thing is sadly certain. Now that the scripts of both *Sutter's Gold* and *An American Tragedy* are published, we can judge their merits for ourselves, and there can be few who would deny their qualities of imagination or regret that, for whatever absurd reasons, Eisenstein's versions were never made.

The Paramount contract was cancelled early in October 1930, five months after Eisenstein's arrival in the United States and seventeen months after his departure from Moscow. As permission to travel to the West had in fact been granted to the three Russians for a maximum period of twelve months, their plans had been faithfully reported to, and approved by, the Soviet film authorities – 'Sovkino' in Moscow, and 'Amkino' in the USA – and their various proposals and contracts had therefore received the full approval of Eisenstein's Soviet masters, who by now had assumed that the team would return home at once.

As the world knows, they did nothing of the kind. There was a plan to pause on the western route to the USSR and make a film in Japan, a proposal that was not only supported by Ivor Montagu but formally approved by Monosson, the Amkino representative in the United States. But Eisenstein wanted passionately to work in Mexico, a country that had gripped his imagination ever since, in 1922, he had designed the sets for the Proletkult's production of Jack London's story *The Mexican*, and now he made it plain to his friends in Hollywood that a film in and about Mexico was the project dearest to his heart. He said as much to Chaplin, who told him that a likely sponsor was the radical novelist, Upton Sinclair.

What happened afterwards is familiar history to every student of the cinema. Sinclair raised the money; Eisenstein, with Alexandrov and Tisse, went to Mexico in December 1930; a draft script was sent to Sinclair who gave it his approval; then Sinclair, seeing the rushes in Hollywood, complained that Eisenstein was over-shooting and spending far too much money in excess of the agreed budget; he called a halt to the production in January 1932, when Eisenstein had shot five of the six planned episodes for the film; Eisenstein never returned to Hollywood (where his 'rushes' had been processed), and saw only part of his footage in New York; he returned to Moscow but his film never followed him; Sinclair, to recover his 'losses', allowed nine films to be quarried from the material shot in Mexico – *Thunder Over Mexico* and *Death Day* (both produced by Sol Lesser), *Time in the Sun* (produced by Eisenstein's biographer, Marie Seton), and six educational shorts made by the Bell and Howell Company. When Eisenstein died in 1948 he had never seen the whole of his Mexican footage, and had never been allowed to edit any of it.

These are the essential and well-known facts. But what really happened, and who was to blame? Ivor Montagu has looked back on the heated affair with calmness and understanding:

'I must make it clear that I quarrelled with Eisenstein over the Mexican project. I could not believe that the enterprise would succeed, and my reason was that Upton Sinclair tried to keep it in his own hands – not for bad motives (for his motives were the best) but partly in order to save money, and partly because his brother-in-law (Hunter Kimbrough), whom he appointed as production manager, knew almost nothing about how films are made and costed. Moreover Eisenstein, strange as it may seem, knew absolutely nothing at all. He knew of film direction. He knew everything that in those days could possibly be known about film technically and artistically. But in the Soviet Union the essential elements of production had been in the hands of others. He had no idea of how much a film would cost in his own country, and even less about its cost anywhere else. But Upton Sinclair had quite fairly asked him that very essential question.

'What could he do? In the event what he did was a singularly silly thing; he went to a bookseller in Hollywood who was well known to us all and who fought with Villa in Mexico, and asked him how much it would cost to make a reasonably priced documentary film in that particular country. Of course he got an absurd answer, but he passed it on to Sinclair in all sincerity. So, when the costs began to rise, Sinclair began to worry, and in his panic he spread the legend that Eisenstein was ludicrously over-shooting and was running up costs that were quite unjustified. All of which was unfair and untrue. According to Sinclair, Eisenstein had shot thirty-five miles of film; but I myself can recall – and I think that most of us who know anything about the cinema can recall – that for a normal feature film in those days we often shot forty-five miles. In any case these were rushes designed to be cut to length in the editing-room. But there was poor ignorant Sinclair, sitting in Hollywood and seeing shot after shot and re-take after re-take (because on remote locations and with your film processed so far away you always shoot more than usual), and saying to himself: "Is this man mad?" Whereas in truth the work was extremely economical, and its total cost would have compared very favourably with such a simple documentary as the British film *Man of Aran*. Eisenstein's *Que Viva Mexico!* was about a whole of a country and its social history, and was full of mass-scenes, whereas *Man of Aran* was concerned with a few people on a tiny island. But the eventual cost of *Man of Aran* was between £17,000 and £20,000; and Eisenstein's completed Mexican project would have cost Sinclair, by his own admission, about £15,000.'

Nobody can any longer doubt the sincerity of Upton Sinclair's motives in arranging the sponsorship of the Mexican expedition. It seemed to him quite disgraceful that a director of such distinction should return home without a single completed film to his credit. Others may have argued that Eisenstein's very presence in California was an insult to the principles of the United States, but for Sinclair the truth was precisely the opposite. It would be disgraceful if Eisenstein were to leave Hollywood without finding at least one person who would help him to make a film of his own choice. That person must, so it seemed, be Sinclair himself, aided and prodded by Mrs Sinclair – two people who knew as much about the economics of film-making as about the road to the moon. The tragedy was that although both sides to the deal had enough contacts in the film industry to pursue the matter realistically, neither of them did so. Why, we may well ask, did Eisenstein go to a bookseller for an estimate of cost when in his friend Chaplin he had the confidence of a man who not only financed his own work with superb accuracy but had recently made a profit of two million dollars? Why did Sinclair appoint as manager of the team in Mexico another man whose knowledge of film-making was minimal – his brother-in-law – when Hollywood was full of those who knew everything that was necessary? Why did neither Sinclair nor Eisenstein insist on a full reconnaissance in Mexico before attempting to measure either the cost or the location problems involved? And later, when Sinclair saw the rushes in a Hollywood viewing theatre, was there really nobody present who could tell him why Eisenstein and Tisse had made so many 'takes' of every shot except the very simplest? Finally, was there no one close enough to Sinclair to tell him that a complete film by Eisenstein for £15,000 was extremely cheap?

As these questions seem unanswerable, the solution to the catastrophe can only lie in the personalities of those involved. Only Eisenstein could have set off for Mexico in such a mood of innocent irresponsibility, and only Upton Sinclair could have followed his initial blunders with others that took him from ignorance via malice to hatred. The documents that Sinclair later placed in the care of the University of Indiana, and which have since been admirably edited in book form make sad and sorry reading. They prove that Sinclair was capable of seeking financial help on the grounds that the film would be both cheap and magnificent, and at the same time write a letter to Eisenstein in Mexico which accused him of excessive extravagance. On one occasion he sent a letter that stated the exact opposite. He promised to send all the material to Moscow, but never in fact did so – though, as proof that perversity can be many-sided, at one point he received a snub from Stalin who declared himself uninterested in the work of a man who was clearly at that time as politically suspect as Comrade Eisenstein. The Indiana documents also show that Eisenstein, the man whose extrovert sense of humour impressed so many people in so many places, easily fell into despair and gloom when it came to the safety of his own work.

But at least Eisenstein was more consistent than his patron. With Tisse and Alexandrov he began shooting in Mexico in December 1930, by which time he had already obtained Sinclair's agreement to a

Que Viva Mexico!, 1931

panorama of Mexican history and the Mexican spirit, and based on a
prologue, six 'novellas', and an epilogue. The prologue, set in Yucatan,
sets up the relationship between past and present which is the theme of
the film. The subject of the first 'novella', called 'Sandyunga', is the
marriage of a young Mexican Indian girl; the second, 'Maguey', is set
at the time of the dictatorship of Diaz, at the beginning of our own
century, and its subject is the tragedy of a wedding between two
young Mexican victims of Spanish colonialism; 'Fiesta' is the title of
the third 'novella', and this too is set in the Diaz period – but now the
central figures are Spanish, and the main character is a picador; the
fourth 'novella', 'Soldarera', and the only one to remain un-shot when
Sinclair ordered the Russians to leave Mexico, was to have reflected
the revolution of 1910 and the fall of Diaz; the epilogue is set in contemporary Mexico, a sequence designed to tie all the threads together.

Shooting *Que Viva Mexico!*

The film ends at a carnival, where 'a cheerful little Indian carefully removes his death-mask and smiles an infectious smile – he impersonates a new, growing Mexico'.

Eisenstein and his two Russian colleagues worked loyally to this treatment, despite problems (which might have been anticipated) with the Mexican authorities, ill-health, and the presence of Upton Sinclair's brother-in-law. Eisenstein was a man who spared neither himself nor others when he was deeply involved in his own creative work. As he was usually charming, so he was frequently ruthless. To have consented to stop production when the estimated budget of £5,000 was first reached and then passed would have been totally out of character. His respect for his paymasters decreased as Sinclair's messages became more hysterical, and his reactions to the rushes increasingly incomprehensible.

Sinclair gave the final order to stop shooting in January 1932. He possessed the film both physically and legally, and Eisenstein's personal position was hopeless. He was permitted to see some of his rushes in New York, and then he returned to Moscow, sad and defeated. So, of course, did Alexandrov and Tisse.

A few years after Eisenstein's death Sinclair presented to the Museum of Modern Art in New York all the footage that had been left unused by Sol Lesser, Marie Seton, and Bell and Howell, and in 1958 Eisenstein's student, Jay Leyda – a distinguished film historian in his own right – reconstructed the original rushes of representative episodes from the prologue and three of the 'novellas'. Leyda's film, simply called *Eisenstein's Mexican Project*, is an honourable piece of scholarship which proves absolutely that when Sinclair cancelled the project he was destroying work of unique potentiality.

The story, fortunately, is not yet ended, for in 1973 all the material that was in New York's Museum of Modern Art was sent to Gosfilmofond (the State Film Archive of the USSR) which in 1974 set up a commission to handle it. Although there were many problems to be resolved – the various cans of film, for instance, were in a chaotic order, nor did they contain the footage used in the 1930s for the film by Sol Lesser, Marie Seton, and Bell and Howell – an article in the magazine *Kino*, and published in 1974, sounded hopeful, emphasizing the 'high photographic quality of the negative'.

4

Frustration and Success

By the spring of 1932 the three Russians had returned home. Eisenstein still believed that the negatives of his Mexican film would soon follow him to Moscow, but he waited for them in vain. Before he left for the West he had pondered a vital question: 'Going abroad offers the final challenge to the creative Soviet worker; to prove whether he can really create outside the Revolution.' In Moscow in 1932 the answer to that challenge seemed to be a sharp negative, and in despair Eisenstein dismissed himself as 'too old' and 'done for'. A year later the young American, Jay Leyda, who was one of his students at the State Institute of Cinematography, asked him why he had so far made no films since his return from Moscow, and received the sharp and anguished reply: 'What do you expect me to do? How can there be a new film when I haven't given birth to the last one?'[1] The sad truth is that his last completed film, *Old and New*, had been shown in 1928, and his next one, *Alexander Nevsky*, was to have its Moscow première exactly ten years later. For a complete decade this man, one of the greatest directors in the history of the cinema, was creatively silent – at least to the general public.

Six months after his return to the Soviet Union he was put in charge of the directors' course at the Institute where he had already been a lecturer before his visit to the West. In his own words it was 'some compensation in all those years when, after the Mexican trauma, I was not able to make a single film'. It may have been a compensation for Eisenstein, but it was a delight and a privilege for his students. One of them, who studied at the Institute several years later, was the director, Grigori Rostotsky:

'He was an extraordinary teacher, who never "talked down" to his students, and never taught them to imitate him. He knew perfectly well that none of us could possibly make films the way he made them, and he quite rightly preferred to develop what was best in each of us. Always he tried to raise each student to his own level, never himself sinking to the level of the person he was speaking to. Whenever you talked with him you became, quite involuntarily, more intelligent, because you were receiving so much new information, new knowledge, new observations.'

To those, and there were many of them, who protested that Eisenstein should be making films instead of theorizing about them, he had his own reply. Marie Seton, who knew him at that time, quotes him as saying: 'All there remains for me to do is analyse what has been done before, and from it to create a synthesis of knowledge; an understanding

With students at the Moscow Film School, 1928

'Buonarotti', 1932. One of the numerous satirical drawings that Eisenstein continued to produce throughout his life

of methods which can be applied to the art of cinematography'; and in a speech at the end of a conference to celebrate the fifteenth anniversary of the Soviet cinema, in 1935, he said: 'I feel it is important to make films, and indeed I intend to make films; but I feel that the making of films must go hand in hand with both intensive theoretical work, and with research.'

Among the students at the Institute were several from outside the Soviet Union, and one of the most senior of them was an Englishman, Herbert Marshall, who has written about Eisenstein's methods of teaching and the remarkable impact he had on those who were learning from him:

'The course at that time lasted four and a half years. Three years were devoted to theoretical and practical work inside the Institute and a year and a half to practical work in the studios and on location. The directors' curriculum covered nearly thirty subjects, including philosophy, political economy, sociology, the fine arts, the history of world cinema and theatre, scenario writing and editing, acting and psychology, theatre, radio and film production, as well as the technical subjects directly concerned with cinema production: photography, lighting, make-up, set designing, studio organization, and so on.

'A student's greatest pride was to work in Eisenstein's Research Group, which was an instrument in the fulfilment of his personal dream: "To lay bare the origins of the nature of artistic creation." I had the privilege to be one of the Group's student-directors for three years.

'Here is a practical example of his teaching method. We were asked to prepare a theatrical production of the assassination scene from Shakespeare's *Julius Caesar*, and the class was divided into four sections, each of which had to stage collectively its own production, planning it on paper in words and designs, and then acting it before the others. It did not have to be a finished production but presented schematically from the director's point of view.

' "If a director can't produce on *one* stage, how can he produce on fifty?" Eisenstein would ask us.

'We had to work to a particular method. First the *General Analysis*: social, historical, political. The collecting of iconographical material, etc. Then *Special Analysis*: theme, plot, style, form, characters, dialogue, images, mood, etc. We established the basic climaxes of "high-spots", then divided the episode into sequences, and the sequences into scenes.

'Next, the organization of the sequence in space: planning of the setting. How, for example, did Shakespeare's theatre deal with the special problem inherent in Act III, Scene I, which is the scene in the street leading to the capitol? How did we ourselves propose to deal with it? We planned the composition of the static in relation to the composition of the dynamic movement within it.

'Then we proceeded to the organization of the sequence in time and space: the composition of the dynamic environment – light, skies, sound, things, people. The composition of the movement of the individual characters and the masses: the *mise-en-scène*. The formless movement of the masses in conflict with the purposeful movement of the conspirators.

'Finally the artistic image of the whole production: the image as the unity of form and content. The development from the seed of the theme to its final external expression. We saw the compositional relationship between the *encircling* of Caesar and the semi-circle of the Senate, the conspirators completing the rest of the circle. The disappearance of Caesar half-way through the play, the semi-circle uncompleted, and the appearance of Caesar's spirit towards the end, completing the circle. Personal assassination cannot kill a social force. Caesar is dead, but Caesarism lives!

'Why did Shakespeare suddenly go into Latin? *"Et tu, Brute!"* Another example, Eisenstein said, of the law relating to the changing of quantity into quality. At the highest tension-point of the sequence (he was always very particular about the tension-points, "That's your close-up point") there is a leap into another dimension. How to express in words the anguish and tragedy of a man receiving his death-blow from his greatest friend? Ordinary language no longer suffices, the leap into the next dimension could be silence or music – or (brilliant stroke of Shakespeare's genius) another tongue. Caesar's mother tongue!

'After this preliminary analysis, each group had to present its *mise-en-scène*. And here we come to Eisenstein's major contribution to the theory of cinema art: his conception of montage, or editing. To Eisenstein editing was something much more than usually conceived.

It was the basic method of artistic composition applied to all works of art; the creation of a higher dimension from the conflict of opposing forces within a lower dimension. The creation of an abstract idea from the collision of concrete ideas. His favourite example was from Chinese hieroglyphs, where:

> Door plus ear = to eavesdrop
> Mouth plus birds = to sing
> Knife plus heart = sorrow

Which is montage in a nutshell, as he used to tell us.

'Now each student had to take his group's theatre production and transform it into his own cinema production. Movements on the stage had to be transformed into movements on the screen – but in terms of screen art. One had to be a development of the other. What *mis-en-scène* is to the expressive movement of the actor, so is the editing to the shots.

'The first historical step had been from theatre to silent film. So we in our turn proceeded from stage sequence to silent film sequence, with minimum sub-titles! Each student, whatever his draughtsmanship, had to sketch every shot in his editing sequence. Eisenstein insisted that every director must be able to explain visual ideas visually to his art director and his cameraman.

'The next stages were to work out the same sequence in sound, and then in colour. So it can be seen from this single example that Eisenstein took his students step by step through the evolution of film art, and the results were always extraordinary. From four different theatrical treatments of the scene came nearly thirty different film treatments, each clearly designed and ready to be executed.

'When we graduated, Eisenstein's final words to us were: "When you come to make your first film, forget all about montage and about me! Here you have learned, but there you must do. And the doing should reveal the learning." '[2]

Eisenstein's talent and passion for teaching spread out far beyond the formal walls of the Institute of Cinematography. Those who can should teach! Grigori Rostotsky was just one of dozens who benefited from Eisenstein's particular passion:

'Sixteen is an age when many young people are seriously thinking about their future and the kind of career they want in life, and I was no exception. But in my own case I was quite certain that I really wanted to be a film director, though I could hardly believe it would ever happen. That word "director" was a word applied to great men – like Eisenstein, whose *Battleship Potemkin* happened to be the first film I had ever seen. Yet despite my lack of self-confidence, and remembering that he and I had met once before, when I was thirteen, I decided to ask him whether in his opinion I had the makings of a film director.

'He agreed to see me, which in itself was of no great significance for he readily agreed to see most people. Nor did he answer my question directly, and indeed I learnt later that to the naïve query, "Can I ever become a film director?" he never gave a straight reply. In my own case his response was to begin teaching me, there and then, and in a most unexpected way. He made me read certain books, he told me to look at particular paintings by particular artists, and he made me listen to selected pieces of music. What he was doing, of course, was to give me a general education in the Arts, and after reading the books or studying the paintings I would be invited to his Moscow flat and we would have long and detailed talks about my own reactions to all those discoveries. Those conversations were a reward as well as a lesson, and as lessons they were the greatest in my whole life. They continued, with the interruption of the war, until I became officially one of Eisenstein's students at the Institute of Cinematography.'

Eisenstein's list of 'unofficial' students was by no means restricted to film-struck teenagers. His advice was frequently sought by men of all ages and of varied experience, including many other professional directors, Mikhail Romm, for example:

'I met Eisenstein only occasionally before his trip to the West, but after his return from Mexico I joined his circle of acquaintances in Moscow. This was the period when he was put in charge of the direc-tors' course at the Institute of Cinematography – which in fact still bases its courses on the curriculum originally worked out by Eisenstein – but in addition to his formal students he collected his informal ones as well, and most of them were film directors who always asked his advice whenever they were beginning a new film; the brothers Sergei and

Georgi Vasiliev, Konstantin Yudin, Friedrich Ermler, and even Pudovkin and Kuleshov. I came to him in 1933 when I was starting my first film, based on Maupassant's story *Boule de Suif*, which Eisenstein knew almost verbatim.

' "What exactly are you doing with the story?" he asked me. "Are you tackling the first part, which is the invasion, or the story of the stage-coach?"

' "The second part. The stage-coach."

' "Then what advice can I possibly give you? I would have done the exact opposite."

' "Perhaps you would," I told him, " but I have every intention of doing the stage-coach."

'I thought that perhaps he might throw me out, but instead he went to his bookshelves. His whole flat in those days consisted of a two-roomed library, with a bedroom attached. There were books everywhere. A huge table was covered in books. An entire wall was filled with bookshelves, and Eisenstein used to sit among the books, on the books, under the books. Now, for my sake, he began to pull various volumes from the shelves: collections of daguerreotypes, histories of costume, and background material of 1880, as though *Boule de Suif* was to be his film and not mine. In a few minutes he had found at least ten superb French editions, and he handed them all to me. "Here," he told me, "read these while I think about it. Then come back in a week's time, and we'll discuss the problem more seriously."

'When I went to see him a week later he had his own ideas and I had mine. He spoke to me very severely.

' "Tell me of your intention and interpretation as director," he said. I began to explain my ideas about the script, but he quickly interrupted me. "No, no," he told me, "I asked for your intentions as director." I found the question more than slightly confusing, and gave him a very fumbling reply.

' "So you don't know what a director's intention means," he said. "Well never mind. Good films have been made without it in the past, and perhaps you'll be lucky. But I absolutely refuse to give you any advice."

'That was the end of the conversation, and for two months I never raised the matter with him. Then, the day before my shooting began, I dared to approach him once more.

'"Sergei Mikhailovich," I said, " tomorrow I start shooting. Please give me some advice. Say something. Anything."

'"Very well then. What's your first shot?"

'"I'm beginning with the simplest of all. A close-up of a pair of boots standing by the door."

'"Excellent. Now this is my advice. You must film those boots in such a way that if you happen to fall under a tram tomorrow night I'd feel justified in taking your shot to the Institute and saying to my students, "Now you can see what a great director we've lost. He took only one shot of a pair of boots, but on the basis of that shot I intend to put those boots in our Museum."

'"Thank you," I said. "I'll do as you say. I'll shoot those boots in exactly that way."

'"But try not to fall under a tram afterwards."

'"I'll do my best. And then? What do I do after that?"

'"Then you must make every shot in that same way, and every film, and every script. And you must continue like that for the rest of your life. That is all the advice I can give you."

'End of discussion! Our next meeting was when *Boule de Suif* was completed and ready for showing. I gave Eisenstein a private viewing, and at the end of it he smiled and said: "I obviously gave you some excellent advice." '

Eisenstein clearly enjoyed such encounters. Nobody ever accused him of false modesty, and he seems to have relished the role of the great man to whom all lesser men came for paternal advice. To later generations, too young to be his official or unofficial students, who know of his skill as a teacher only at second-hand, those years between his return from Mexico and his first work on *Alexander Nevsky* appear as a sad creative desert. What happened to Eisenstein the film-maker, and why did it happen? The first part of that question is easy to answer. The second is much more complicated.

What is clear is that despite Eisenstein's despair at the collapse of *Que Viva Mexico!* he had every intention of resuming his creative career in his own country. During the winter of 1932/3 he worked on a satirical comedy to be called *M M M – Maxim Maximovich Maximov –* in which 'the Russian boyars would be transplanted into the life of modern Moscow'. The shooting-script was completed and many of the actors had been chosen (including Maxim Strauch) when the project was 'postponed' by the new administrator of the Soviet cinema, Boris Shumyatsky. Nor did anything come of two other counter-proposals during the same period: that he should direct a musical, and that he should make a film with Paul Robeson about the Haitian revolution.

In 1933 he made detailed notes and drawings for *Moscow*, whose theme was to be four hundred years of the city's history, intercut with the story of several generations of a working family. In 1934 he considered a second idea about the same city, to be called *Moscow the Second*, and to be made in conjunction with Nathan Zarkhi's play of the same title, about the relationship between a worker-hero and a public statue erected in his honour. Both proposals were turned down by Shumyatsky's office as being counter to the current needs of the Soviet cinema.

In Moscow with Paul Robeson and Herbert Marshall, 1934

In 1934 Paul Robeson came to Moscow, and with Eisenstein he discussed not only the Haitian proposal, but also an adaptation of A. K. Vinogradov's novel *The Black Consul*. Nothing came of these ideas, and two others that Eisenstein was considering in 1934 were also abandoned. Only one potential film of this period went beyond the planning, scripting, and casting stages, and it was called *Bezhin Meadow*.

The author of its original script, commissioned by the Young Communist League, was Alexander Rzheshevsky, who had worked with Pudovkin on the film *A Simple Case*. Its origin was a story by Turgenev, but the core of Rzheshevsky's scenario was the tale of a young village boy, called Stepok in the film, who had organized the local 'young pioneers' to guard the harvest of the farm 'collective'

Bezhin Meadow, 1935

each night, thereby frustrating the plans of his own father to sabotage it. In the film's climax, the father kills the son.

The shooting of *Bezhin Meadow*, which was to be Eisenstein's first sound film, began in May 1935, with Eduard Tisse once more as cameraman, but in October Eisenstein contracted smallpox, followed by a long convalescence in the Caucasus and a severe bout of influenza. By this time sixty per cent of the film had been shot, which was enough to persuade Shumyatsky that *Bezhin Meadow* was not the kind of product that was needed in the Soviet Union at that time. He made several criticisms, and Isaac Babel was called in to revise the script. In January 1937 Eisenstein once again collapsed with severe influenza, and in March Shumyatsky finally ordered that production on the film should be stopped. Eisenstein later described the cancellation of *Bezhin Meadow* as 'one of the most painful experiences of my whole life'.

Bezhin Meadow, 1935

There can be no simple explanation of the fact that Eisenstein failed to complete a single film during the first six years after his return from Mexico. The political situation, the economics of the Soviet film industry, personal rivalries and jealousies, and above all Eisenstein's own depression after the Mexican episode . . . all these factors were involved in varying degrees and at various times. The familiar theory that it was all due to Shumyatsky is both tempting and superficial, and John Grierson was one of Eisenstein's acquaintances who preferred to place the emphasis on his personality:

'It is never reasonable to discuss an artist's work without also considering him as a human being, trying to relate the quality of the humanity to the quality of the work. In Eisenstein this relationship has always struck me as strangely inconsistent. Superficially he was always good to meet, and on public occasions he behaved extremely well. But he was also a man who carried within himself some deep hurt, and with it an inability to take life's slings and arrows as easily as most of us. This capacity to be hurt, which may have had its origins in his early dependence on his mother, seemed to fill his working life with a constant sequence of frustrations, and not all of them can be explained by the theory that he was an idealist who worked in a cynical society. Certainly there were terrible frustrations in his own country – and the suppression of *Bezhin Meadow* was probably the worst of them – but also there were frustrations nearly everywhere else. *Battleship Potemkin* had been shown in Berlin without much fuss, but there was a considerable struggle to screen it elsewhere in Germany. In the public cinemas of Britain it was not shown for several years after its completion. I well remember his bitterness at the manner in which several of his films were cut in the Netherlands, and there were his more famous failures in Hollywood and Mexico.'

When Eisenstein had left Moscow in 1929 he was by no means uncriticized in the Soviet Union. In retrospect, and especially to Western eyes, he may seem to have been the most exciting of the Soviet directors, but this was not the unanimous view in Moscow at that time. His work was as frequently attacked for its failure to communicate to a popular and uninformed audience as it was praised for its professional inventiveness and its evidence of a superb visual imagination, and his last two films had been more vigorously criticized than either *Strike* or *Battleship Potemkin*. His reputation, far from increasing, was arguably declining in 1929, a situation that was later to be reflected in the 1932 edition of the *Soviet Encyclopedia*, which complained that in *October* and *Old and New* Eisenstein 'in spite of his great skill failed to analyse in any depth the most decisive stages of the Socialist Revolution, allowing himself to be side-tracked by formalistic experimentation'.

The reason for his journey to the West had been to study the technique of synchronized sound, but in his absence several sound films were made in the Soviet Union and by directors of considerable distinction. In 1931 Dziga Vertov made *Enthusiasm*, Nikolai Ekk made *Road to Life*, Yakov Protazanov made *Tommy*, Yutkevich made *Golden Mountains*, and Kozintsev and Trauberg were co-directors of *Alone*, which had an original score by Shostakovich. Dovzhenko's *Ivan* was shown in the autumn of 1932, and soon after Eisenstein's return from Mexico Pudovkin was to begin work on his *Deserter*. The revolution – artistic, technical, and industrial – which the development of synchronized sound brought to the Soviet cinema was well advanced by the spring of 1932. It had taken place in Eisenstein's absence, and he had played no part in it. He had left his country during a crucial period in the development of its film industry, he returned without completing a film of his own, and his most valuable contribution to the development of the sound film was still his share in a manifesto, called *Sound and Image*, which was also signed by Pudovkin and Alexandrov, and had been published as long ago as 1928.[3]

The attitude to the cinema of the government of the Communist Party had been modified in Eisenstein's absence. The importance of Boris Shumyatsky is that he was put in administrative control of the industry during the period of its most rapid expansion, when new studios were being opened not only in Moscow and Leningrad, but in regional centres like Tiflis and Kiev. His qualifications were those of an organizer, not of an artist, and in encouraging work which may nowadays seem tedious and mechanical he was merely carrying out the declared policies of the Party and the Government. The 'new' Soviet films gave to the actor a greater prominence than before and related everything to the basic principle of socialist realism. Although a personal antagonism seems to have existed between Shumyatsky and Eisenstein, it is also true that many of the experiments that Eisenstein had introduced into his silent films, as well as his work in the theatre during the early 1920s, would have been actively discouraged in the Soviet film industry of the 1930s. Eisenstein, at least in public, seems to have accepted the new policy as both inevitable and desirable. In a speech opening a conference of the Union of Cinematograph Workers to celebrate the fifteenth anniversary of the Soviet cinema in January 1935 he said:

'To many people the progressive development of the Soviet cinema seems to have ended. But this is not of course the truth of the matter. One very important fact is being forgotten by the eager supporters of our old silent films, who find themselves puzzled that so much of our current work resembles, at least on the surface, the products of other nations. If it is true that the immediate brilliance of much of our work (which is a quality that so many of our foreign friends have come to expect) has been often diluted recently, then the reason is that our industry . . . is entirely concerned with exploring and deepening the ideological aspects of the issues and the problems that are the real content of each film. . . . The Soviet cinema is passing through a new period of more open Bolshevization. . . .'[4]

During this period it was Alexandrov who prospered when Eisenstein was silent. Applying his new knowledge of Hollywood to his work in Moscow he made a series of very successful musicals, which turned his wife, Lyubov Orlova, into the first Soviet 'talkie' film-star, and gave him a Grand Prix at the Venice Film Festival in 1934.

The Anniversary Conference of 1935 was a sad occasion for Eisenstein.[5] Despite his opening speech (or in some cases perhaps because of it) he was publicly teased by several of his fellow directors, including Yutkevich, Sergei Vasiliev, and Dovzhenko. It was Dovzhenko who set the mood in a speech of quite extraordinary passion:

'When I listened to Eisenstein's statement I began to fear that this man has far too much knowledge, and that his head is so clear about everything that he'll probably never make another film. If I knew all that he knows I would quite literally die! . . . I'm quite sure that in more ways than one his erudition is killing him. No! Excuse me, I meant to use some other word. I should have said "disorganizing" him. . . .'

Then, facing Eisenstein, he added forcefully: 'Sergei Mikhailovich, if you fail to make a film within twelve months at the latest, I beg you never to make one at all. We will have no need of it, and neither will you. . . .'

It was a speech that must have come straight from the heart. So, in a different way, did Kuleshov's emotional defence of his old friend and colleague: 'You have all spoken of him . . . as though he is a corpse that you are burying before its time. For myself, I must tell him, as someone who is still very much alive, and whom I love and admire greatly . . . "Dear Sergei Mikhailovich, please remember that nobody ever explodes from an excess of knowledge, but only from a surfeit of envy." '

The climax of the Fifteenth Anniversary celebrations was a presentation of honours at the Bolshoi Theatre, and those who expected Eisenstein's name to be announced had to wait a long time. The Order of Lenin, the highest of the honours, was awarded to Shumyatsky, Pudovkin, Dovzhenko, Kozintsev, and the brothers Vasiliev. Two of Shumyatsky's assistants were among those who received the second award, the Order of the Red Banner of Labour, and Alexandrov and Vertov were given the Order of the Red Star. The Award of People's Artist was then announced, and still there was no mention of Eisenstein. His turn came even later and lower, when with Tisse and Kuleshov he received the minor Award of Honoured Art Worker. It was a formal statement of his position in the Soviet film industry in 1935. There were many present on that occasion who had hoped and expected that he would receive the Order of Lenin, just as there were probably those who argued privately that a director who had not made a film for five years should be given nothing at all. But the occasion was a celebration of fifteen years' work, and during that time Eisenstein had made films that were surely as good as the best of Pudovkin or Dovzhenko.

During this period of disappointment his career received little help from his personal health. Several bouts of acute influenza, a period of rest caused by exhaustion, as well as attacks of ptomaine poisoning and smallpox, all removed him physically from active work, and often at times when his creative life demanded that he should be fully fit. The profound depression that followed the collapse of *Que Viva Mexico!* could also be fairly described as a form of illness.

His personality also remained an obstacle to his professional prosperity. After two and a half years abroad he was out of tune with the temper of Soviet Russia in the early 1930s, and it was not in his nature to compromise with it. Marie Seton, who met Eisenstein on several occasions during those years, has made the point admirably in her biography:

'His retreat into books and research widened the gulf between him and his fellow directors – Pudovkin, Dovzhenko, Kozintsev, Trauberg, and others – who spent much of their free time in social activities . . . aimed at furthering the development of socialist society and bringing culture to the masses. . . . (Eisenstein) seldom went out except to teach, attend a theatre, film, or concert. Inevitably many people in Russia concluded that since he had been abroad Eisenstein had no interest in anything but himself and his own ideas. . . .

'. . . It would have been good if the Old Man would do what other Soviet artists found extremely helpful: talk over their ideas with their fellow artists and, if necessary, discuss the problems freely with some members of the Central Committee of the Communist Party.

'But for Eisenstein it was impossible to follow such a course. He would not know, as he explained, how to begin to express his ideas to an official, or a political leader.'[6]

When Boris Shumyatsky ordered the cancellation of *Bezhin Meadow* he explained his reasons in a statement published in *Pravda* in March 1937:

'From the beginning Eisenstein associated his work on *Bezhin Meadow* with the need for a complete reassessment of his own artistic methods, and indeed he had promised to recognize the new principles that had been developed in the years of his silence. Moreover the effects of that silence were made more serious by the fact that both the shape and the content of his last film, *Old and New*, contained many basic mistakes.

'He could hardly ignore the fact that the most recent works of

Soviet art, in all the media, have become more and more politically responsible. Because of this he readily declared his intention of working in the new way, in the true spirit of socialist realism, and of correcting his serious mistakes of the past.

'Yet despite this, Eisenstein was enthusiastic about Rzheshevsky's script, even though it contained serious flaws. . . . The plot was badly constructed and didactic, the characters were poorly drawn, and the entire script lacked the essential drive that gives a film its true ideological and artistic purpose. . . . Unfortunately Eisenstein paid no attention to the suggestions we all gave him. . . . From the very first shot it was clear that he was treating his subject-matter both subjectively and arbitrarily. . . . He should have presented our enemies as the opponents of both the people and of socialism, but he preferred to turn them into creatures living in a world of religious mythology that is a million years away from the ideas of our own time. . . . He transformed the personality of the chief of the political section into a man with a totally expressionless face, a big beard, and features that are indisputably biblical. . . . Moreover the young hero, the pioneer Stepok, was presented in pale and luminous tones, with the face of some kind of holy youth whose fate was already decided by a supernatural destiny. Indeed in many of the shots the lighting is so contrived that this pale boy in his white shirt seems to be wrapped up in a halo. . . .

'. . . The film's conception is not in any true sense based on the class struggle, but on a conflict of more elemental forces, or a fight between "good and evil". Eisenstein goes out of his way to show the crazy, bestial hatred of some of his characters, and the "holiness" of the others. . . .

'. . . Eisenstein wanted to make *Bezhin Meadow* because it seemed to be a good opportunity for his academic exercises. . . . Therefore he intentionally diluted the film's ideological content. . . . On several occasions he verbally conceded the truth of our criticisms, but his work continued to ignore them totally.

'. . . He was so sure of his own unanswerable authority that he completely declined to respect public opinion. He refused to study a world of which he was ignorant, preferring to rely on his own academic erudition. And in the end he discovered that the task was quite beyond him.'[7]

A few days later Eisenstein wrote a long 'self-criticism' that was published in *Sovietskoye Iskusstvo* in April 1935. Some of its main points were these:

'By nature I have a tremendous urge to generalize, but mine is not really the kind of generalization that our Marxist principles of realism have taught us to understand. Sometimes this generalization in my work destroys the basic detail, leading me into an area of uncommitted abstractions. This was by no means true of *Battleship Potemkin*, where in a single episode of the revolution of 1905 I managed to include everything that was most typical of that particular phase of our revolutionary struggle.

'But such was not the case in *Bezhin Meadow*. Feeble generalizations pushed the entire visual imagery of the film in the direction of stylized characters and traditional mythology – the father as Pan, the peasant as Samson, and the young pioneer as a "boy novice". . . . The full-blooded and many-sided nature of the vital and tragic class collision slithered lamely into a melodrama expressed in simple terms of "black and white". The reality of the class struggle was transformed into a generalized and cosmic battle between "the forces of good and evil".

'The criticism of my colleagues have made me see very clearly the film's mistaken aims. . . . So now I must seriously reconsider my own outlook, applying a true Marxist approach to my subject-matter. . . . My future work must be of only one kind: heroic in spirit, forceful in content, and very popular in technique. Whether it be set in 1917 or 1937 it must help the victorious advance of Socialism.'[8]

Those words were probably written as much in irony as in repentance. Eisenstein's belief in a socialist society was as genuine as his support for the system of government in his own country, but he was also an artist at odds with the 'establishment' of the day, and possibly even at odds with his own time. To confess that he was wrong, or at least mistaken, was a gesture that did him little damage as an artist. If it affected his creative work at all, it did so constructively, making his personal position easier than it might have been otherwise.

Many of the foreign visitors who met him in the 1930s are agreed that he was cautious and subdued.[9] Marie Seton was one of them, and another was Léon Moussinac who met him several times in 1933 and again in 1937. In 1933 he found that his 'attitude had changed, and that his good humour was forced', and in 1937, shortly after the cancellation of *Bezhin Meadow*, he tried to avoid any mention of contemporary politics; 'he wanted to rest, and he complained of his heart'. Basil Wright, who visited Moscow in the following year, failed to make contact with him, even though he had the best possible letters of introduction and was a man with whose work Eisenstein must have been in sympathy. The German writer Lion Feuchtwanger met him during the production of *Bezhin Meadow*, and noted not only his fears that more and more cuts would be ordered, but also his anxiety when he began to realize that Isaac Babel, who was working with him on the revised script, was a potential victim of Stalin's cultural purge.

Eisenstein's work as a teacher remained a compensation. In a letter to Jay Leyda dated 1 February 1937 he referred to his theoretical work as 'the really most important of what I have to do'. It is of course true that his teaching and his theoretical writing were matters of deep concern to him, and it is almost literally true that on his return from Mexico he had sought solace by burying himself in his books. It is equally true that he was often unhappy, and indeed he later confessed that the 1930s had a 'grey atmosphere' caused largely by 'the attempt to force us all into a straitjacket of conformity'. In truth it was worse than that, and Eisenstein was well aware of the fate of many of his close friends and colleagues: Isaac Babel; Meyerhold, the man he most admired in the theatre; Konstantin Eggert, the film director; Sergei Tretyakov, the dramatist and script-writer. Mayakovsky, who had shared so much of the excitement of the early 1920s, committed suicide.

Eisenstein survived. His survival was no doubt due to a variety of causes, not the least of them being Stalin's personal liking for him as a man, as well as his respect for Lenin's views about the importance of the cinema as an art form in a socialist society. Eisenstein was also happy with his writing, his students, and his friendships, and all of these helped to sustain him. His statement to the Fifteenth Anniversary Conference and his public apology for the 'errors' of *Bezhin Meadow* were probably the gestures of a man willing to concede a tactical defeat as long as his strategy won him the ultimate victory. What is significant, and most to his credit, is his refusal in practice to produce work that he personally despised. He may well, as Shumyatsky claimed, have agreed verbally to criticisms made during the production of *Bezhin Meadow* and have offered to change the film accordingly. But in practice he did nothing of the kind, insisting to himself that the film would be made as he wanted it, or it would never be made at all. In the event it was left uncompleted.

Yet Shumyatsky's decision to suspend its production was not the end of *Bezhin Meadow*, whose story was dramatically resumed nearly twenty years later. What happened then has been described by Eisenstein's contemporary, Sergei Yutkevich:

'Not only was *Bezhin Meadow* never finished but, as far as we knew, all the prints and all the original negative were destroyed during the war by bomb damage. All that seemed to remain were Eisenstein's own general "treatment" and two different versions of the script. Even these were not as valuable as they may seem, for Eisenstein was never a believer in a fixed and unchangeable scenario that indicated every shot in precise detail. It was therefore extremely difficult to imagine exactly what he had in his mind, and still less the precise shape of every shot. So when Eisenstein died in 1948, *Bezhin Meadow* seemed lost for ever, or so we all thought. But happily we were wrong.

'I myself was made head of a committee appointed to administer Eisenstein's legacy, and when we began to publish his writings in several volumes we were inevitably concerned to find the best and most suitable illustrations. It was in the course of his search for these that a young film historian, Naum Kleiman, came across small clips from nearly every shot of *Bezhin Meadow*. He found them in the archive kept by Eisenstein's widow, Pera Attasheva. What happened was that during the shooting of the film he had for some unexplained reason given orders for several frames to be cut from each roll of film, and these frames – about a thousand of them altogether – gave us our first knowledge of *Bezhin Meadow* in its plastic form. Naum Kleiman had the clips extended into lengths of one or two metres each, and he and I began to use these bits of film in an attempt to restore something of what Eisenstein had managed to achieve.

'We agreed to make two versions, and the first of them would consist of the frames assembled together in sequence, relying on both versions of the script. But I was eager to do more than that. I wanted to make another version altogether, by trying to edit creatively those apparently dead bits of film. I remembered that Eisenstein had been very fond of Harlequinades, and often quoted the sequence in which Pierrot and Harlequin are hacked into little pieces. Then, inevitably, the Fairy enters the stage and sprinkles them with the magic water of life. The pieces come together and the characters begin to act once again. So I wondered whether we could sprinkle those little pieces of *Bezhin Meadow* with the magic water of film editing, and to convey at least a part of what Eisenstein had intended in his film.

'I tried the experiment, basing my work mainly on the first version of the script by Alexander Rzheshevsky, and using only one episode from the second. Of course it was extremely risky of me to attempt such a thing, and the only reason why I did it at all was based on a private joke; Eisenstein, an editor of real genius, once told me that I was the only other good editor in existence! So with this conceited thought in mind I tried to edit those bits of film as Eisenstein himself might have done. I began to sort out their sequence, capture their rhythm, discover the subtle visual connection between each one and the next.

'We needed music, and were lucky to have the services of Boris Volsky, who had recorded the sound-track for both parts of *Ivan the Terrible* and was an experienced sound director as well as a musician in his own right. Together he and I devised a musical background from the Third and Fifth Symphonies of Prokofiev, who had written the scores for both *Ivan the Terrible* and *Alexander Nevsky*. I hope our experiment succeeded, and that at least the world could see – or at any rate imagine from our imperfect shadow – what Eisenstein had intended in his amazing film. At the very least *Bezhin Meadow* is no longer a mere myth.'

It is of course unfair to judge *Bezhin Meadow* on the only available evidence – Rzheshevsky's script and Babel's amendments, Eisenstein's notes, and the loyal re-creation of Yutkevich and Kleiman. A few points only can be made with certainty: the excellence of Tisse's camerawork and especially his 'mood' photography, the vicious atmosphere of violence and terror, Eisenstein's deeply personal approach as reflected by the relationship of the boy-hero and his father, and strong hints in the lighting and composition of images that Shumyatsky had some truth on his side when he wrote of the heroic and biblical handling of father and son. The probability is that *Bezhin Meadow* would have been a great film, but we will never be able to prove it.

Boris Shumyatsky had ordered the suspension of *Bezhin Meadow* in March 1937. Within a year the situation had completely changed for Shumyatsky, for Eisenstein, and for the Soviet cinema. Shumyatsky was removed from his post and Eisenstein had begun work on *Alexander Nevsky*. At its Moscow première in November 1938 he expressed his personal thanks to Stalin for making it possible, and in 1939, together with Alexandrov, he received the Order of Lenin. The dark days were apparently over.

As soon as Eisenstein had accepted *Alexander Nevsky* as his next film he quickly broke the news to all his friends. One of them was Mikhail Romm:

'It was the summer of 1937, and from Eisenstein himself, that I first heard of the proposal to make a film about Alexander Nevsky. We had houses next door to each other in the country at Kratov, and one afternoon he called to me from the garden fence.

'"I've got a choice of two subjects for my next film," he said. "Either Ivan Susanin or Alexander Nevsky." I was surprised that he should be thinking of going so far back in history, and I told him so.

'"Oh I knew you'd regard both those ideas as irrelevant and out of date," he said. "But why should you? What is it that makes you always regard history as something dead and useless? I happen to know that despite what you say I'll enjoy doing it. So . . . which would you choose, Ivan Susanin or Alexander Nevsky?"

'"I'd like some time to think about it."

'"All right, if you insist. But please don't take too long." He smiled, and I knew that he expected a reply there and then. So I frowned for a few seconds and then said: "Susanin".

'"Why?" He looked surprised.

'"Because for one thing you have a good plot, the dramatic story of a peasant. Then the period of history is well researched and well documented. But Alexander Nevsky is largely a mystery."

"'Precisely!'" Eisenstein said, with an odd look of truimph on his face. "And that is exactly why it appeals to me. Nobody knows much about him, and so nobody can possibly find fault with me. Whatever I do the historians and the so-called "consultants" won't be able to argue with me. They all know as well as you and I do that the evidence is slim. So I'm in the strongest possible position, for everything I do must be right. Apart from that there's one aspect of Nevsky as a subject that particularly appeals to me."

"'What aspect is that?'"

"'Tell me how much you know about the military order of the Teutonic Knights.'"

"'Very little.'"

"'Then let me explain it to you.'" He picked up a small branch and began to draw on the soil with all the excitement of a small boy on a beach. "They used to fight in the form of a wedge, like this. Imagine this wedge as a vast regiment of men, all on horseback, all in heavy armour, their lances at the ready. Now they move forward, like a tank. Then they cut up the enemy army, exactly like a tank." He stood up, rather proudly, as though he had created a work of art, or perhaps stumbled on some profound philosophical truth. "Now, Mikhail Ilyich?"

"'I find it extremely interesting,' I told him, without much cnthusiasm. "But to make a successful film I'd have thought you needed more than a handful of authentic documents and the idea of an army of men who operate like a tank."

"'Not at all," he replied, quite unruffled. "I can invent all the rest. I'll find an actor, and cast him as Alexander Nevsky, and the whole world will soon believe that the real Nevsky was just like my actor. If I choose a fat actor, then Nevsky was fat. If I have a thin actor, then he was thin. Then and now, always and for ever."

'He laughed loudly, and rubbed out the Teutonic tank from the flower-bed.'

Alexander Nevsky was made with extraordinary speed. Eisenstein began work on it with his co-author, Pyotr Pavlenko, in the late summer of 1937, shooting began in the spring of 1938, and the completed film was ready by November of the same year, five months ahead of schedule – an achievement made easier by the presence of a co-director, Dmitri Vasiliev. Eduard Tisse was the principle cameraman, and the music was composed by Prokofiev. Nikolai Cherkasov reluctantly agreed to play the part of Alexander Nevsky, and must have felt ashamed about his earlier indecision when he was awarded the Order of Lenin for his part in the film.

Alexander Nevsky was conceived as a piece of history with contemporary overtones, and was first shown only two months after the Munich Pact. The defeat of the invading Teutonic Knights by the forces of Alexander Nevsky in the thirteenth century became by implication a comment on Nazi aggression and, more ominously, proved to be a prophecy of what was to happen in Soviet Russia three years later. *Alexander Nevsky* immediately became Eisenstein's greatest success both with the public and the critics, in his own country and overseas; but the sharp pinch

At work on *Alexander Nevsky*, 1938

of history was to bruise him once more when it was withdrawn from general circulation during the period between the signing of the Nazi–Soviet agreement and the invasion of the USSR in 1941. The success of *Alexander Nevsky* was well deserved. Less obviously personal than most of Eisenstein's previous work it was also more disciplined and, in the most literal sense, more popular. In the battle on the ice – filmed near the Mosfilm studios in a July heatwave – it proved that he had lost none of his old skill as a director of mass movement and mass action. In Prokofiev he found a partner with whom he could have a creative collaboration as close and as productive as that with Eduard Tisse. Prokofiev shared Eisenstein's passion for hard work, which was another reason why the film was finished ahead of schedule. The two men would watch a rough-cut of a particular sequence in the cutting-room until midnight; Prokofiev made detailed timings from his stop-

Alexander Nevsky. The Battle on the Ice, a photograph taken during a Moscow heatwave, on 25 June 1938

watch, and twelve hours later would deliver his suggested music. It was Eisenstein's first collaboration with a composer and it was Prokofiev's first original score for the cinema. It remains indisputably one of the greatest film scores ever written, and Eisenstein himself had no doubts about their mutual achievement: 'I could say much about the unity of sound and vision in *Alexander Nevsky*, and certainly in some of the sequences made with Prokofiev I have achieved the kind of result I used to dream about years and years ago.'

After *Alexander Nevsky* he endured another period of public inactivity, working hard enough but with nothing to show for it except his writing and his teaching. With Alexander Fadeyev he began to write a script about the Civil War in the Crimea and then 'postponed' it because of another idea that excited him much more – an epic film based on the construction of the Ferghana Canal in Uzbekistan, which he described in a letter to Ivor Montagu as 'a great tragedy of the struggle of human beings among themselves and the hopeless struggle of humanity against deserts and sands'.[10] Tisse would be the principal cameraman and Eisenstein hoped that once again Prokofiev would compose the music. Shooting had begun in Uzbekistan in the autumn of 1939 when the production was halted for reasons that remain uncertain but which are probably connected with the state of Europe at the beginning of another World War.

In 1940, as part of a government policy to put Russia's best film directors in positions of creative authority – Dovzhenko, for example, was assigned to the studios in Kiev – Eisenstein became the artistic head of Mosfilm in Moscow, a position that once again brought him into contact with Mikhail Romm:

'Eisenstein took his new responsibilities extremely seriously. He regularly visited the stages and the cutting-rooms, and he often came to see me on the set of my latest film, *The Dream*. The principal part of one of the main sets was a bridge, and the floor of the studio was knee-deep in water when Eisenstein decided to inspect it all and hopefully to give it the Artistic Director's stamp of approval. "Give me some boots," he shouted, "I want to see what Romm is up to." We gave him the boots, and he splashed through the water, discussing the set and the décor.

'I doubt whether the quality of our work was really very important to him on such occasions, but he enjoyed walking round, wandering about in the water, looking at this and that, and generally playing the part of the Artistic Boss of the studio. He made a few comments, was helpful enough, and then left. The best way to describe his remarks is to call them "amusing". In the course of the production he visited every set and watched part of the shooting of almost every sequence. If he was pleased with what he saw, he made a joke. If there was something he disliked he still made a joke, but it was much more caustic. Often he left the poor director guessing whether he was pleased or otherwise.

'This of course was typical of Eisenstein's general personality. His own thought processes were extremely complicated, and it was usually a tough exercise in intelligence and imagination to understand his real meaning. For anyone who made the effort it was a great pleasure to talk with him and to hear what he had to say. But unfortunately his erudition and his sharp wit were poor helpmates to clarity.'

During the same year he returned to the theatre for the first time in seventeen years. On 1 November 1940 a production of Wagner's *Die Walküre*, designed and directed by Eisenstein, opened at the Bolshoi Theatre in Moscow. 'I made all the sets myself,' he wrote to Jay Leyda, 'and I had great fun in doing the production. Pity you couldn't see it.' Shortly afterwards he was working on draft scripts for a film to be based on the life of the man who is generally regarded as Russia's greatest poet – Alexander Pushkin. It was an idea which, like so many others down the years, had entered his mind, nestled there, and then left to give way to something else that seemed for the present to be more compulsive. This time the new captor of Eisenstein's creative brain was Ivan IV, Grand Duke of Moscow and Tsar of Russia, who came to the throne in 1533 at the age of three and is commonly known as 'the Terrible'.[11] Once again Mikhail Romm was one of the first to hear of his latest ambition:

'By this time our mutual eminence had been turned upside down. Eisenstein was still the Head of Productions at the Mosfilm Studios but I held a post in the Government as the Minister concerned with cinematography. I was therefore technically his superior, and though

Ivan the Terrible. Drawing by Eisenstein for the scene at Anastasia's grave, 1942

in his case I could never feel able to exert my authority in any of the discussions we had together, I saw him quite frequently in my office at the Ministry. One day he came to me and said that somebody in the Government – and he quoted the name far higher than my own – had suggested a film about Ivan Grozny, Ivan the Terrible. I got the distinct impression from the way he spoke that this senior person was proposing, through Eisenstein as an intermediary, that I myself should leave my job and direct such a film. Ivan had always interested me as a character, and I was in any case particularly interested in that period of Russian history. I said as much to Eisenstein. "I'll take it on with pleasure," I added.

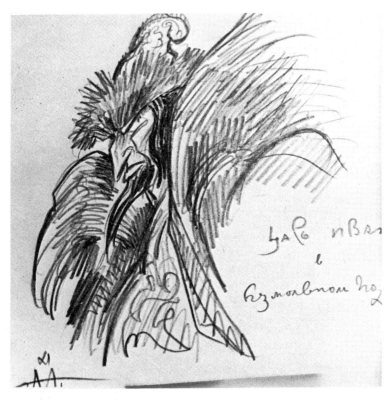

Ivan the Terrible. Drawing by Eisenstein of Tsar Ivan IV

'But this was not the idea at all and Eisenstein, looking slightly embarrassed before the Minister, explained very quickly that *he* was to make the film, not Mikhail Romm.

'"More history," I asked him, "and so soon after *Alexander Nevsky*?"

'"Exactly. More history. But there are many reasons for making this particular film at the present time." He was right, of course, but I made no comment, and let him continue. "I want to write my own scenario, and design the sets and the costumes – everything. I'll begin with some of the drawings. I'll begin immediately."

'In fact he began work on *Ivan the Terrible* the very next day, and I saw his first outlines and sketches about a month later. The film was conceived in three parts, and Part One was shot at Alma Ata, East of Tashkent in Central Asia, which was the headquarters of Mosfilm during its wartime evacuation from Moscow. Part Two was completed after the war, but Part Three, very sadly, was never made. If it had been, there was every chance that Mikhail Romm, a former Minister in a Soviet government, might have played the part of Queen Elizabeth I of England.'

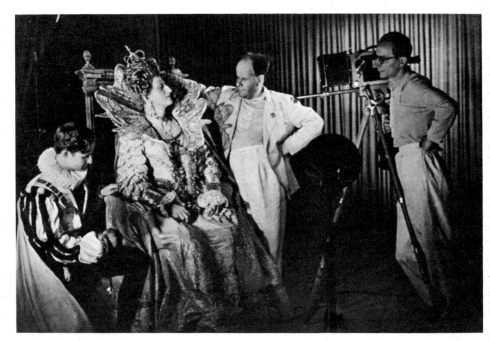

Mikhail Romm being tested for the part of Queen Elizabeth I of England, for *Ivan the Terrible* (Part III)

Eisenstein wrote down, in simpler language than usual, some of his intentions:

'The basic idea of the film is to show Ivan in the full context of his tremendous efforts on behalf of the Russian state in and around the city of Moscow, and I must say quite bluntly that a great deal of what he did, and the ways in which he did it, were as bloody as they were grandiose. Nor shall we ignore a single drop of all the blood that was shed during the life of Ivan IV. Our aim is not to whitewash but to explain.

'In this way, without hiding anything or modifying anything in the story of *Ivan the Terrible*, and also without denying his extraordinary and romantic popular image, we hope to present him, complete and as he truly was, to cinema audiences throughout the world.'

The shooting of *Ivan the Terrible* began in April 1943, using the former Palace of Culture at Alma Ata as a studio – but in the evenings only, when electricity could be spared from the more urgent needs of war-

On location for *Ivan the Terrible*, 1943

time industry. Eduard Tisse photographed the exteriors for Part One,
but the cameraman for the interiors – the bulk of the film – was Andrei
Moskvin. Eisenstein asked Prokofiev to write the musical score, and
the composer arrived willingly at Alma Ata from the Georgian capital
of Tiflis, where he had been working on his opera, *War and Peace*.
Nikolai Cherkasov played the part of Ivan, Ludmila Tselikovskaya
was the Tsarina Anastasia, and the distinguished theatre actress,
Serafima Birman, played Euphrosina, the aunt of Ivan. Many years
later she spoke of the days when she worked, for the first and the last
time, with Eisenstein:

'I had been a pupil of the great theatre director, Konstantin Stanislavsky, and by conviction I am an actress who prefers to work in the theatre
than in the cinema – though for some reason as a member of the
audience I usually get more pleasure from the cinema.

'So it was strange that Eisenstein should have asked me to play in
Ivan the Terrible, especially as his attitude towards my own previous
work, or indeed the work of any actor trained by Stanislavsky, had
always been extremely sceptical. He once expressed the opinion that
our art was no better than froth, and a froth that was not by any means
from champagne; it came, so he said, from something much cheaper

Eisenstein working with Prokofiev at Alma Ata, 1943

Nikolai Cherkasov as Tsar Ivan IV

than that, like beer, or even soap. He preferred his drinks to be "pure and clear", without froth of any kind whatever. No doubt he said all this in the heat of the moment, but the fact remains that it was the basic cause of a great deal of friction between us when we were working at Alma Ata. I used to call this period my "Euphrosiniad", which he took as a rather nasty insult. I often made him angry, and I know that sometimes I seriously upset him. Then, in his turn, he would say or do something that hurt me just as much.

'So the filming of *Ivan the Terrible* was for me a time of shadow as well as light, and I still think that the shadow was probably more powerful than the light. Yet, in retrospect, I doubt whether those shadows were real ones, for Eisenstein worked with such a genuine passion, such spontaneous inspiration, and ultimately with such true comradeship that to distress him unnecessarily, as some of us did, was to slap his superb talents in the face. For the truth is that despite it all we loved this man, but with a love that we never expressed in words, either to him or to ourselves, but by working long and hard, by day,

Ivan the Terrible. Serafima Birman as Euphrosinia, and Pyotr Kadochnikov as her son

by night, and often on our so-called holidays as well. So we agreed to do the most extraordinary things for him; for instance Cherkasov, in the Kazan sequence, had to wear a very heavy metal costume, and he willingly stood in it on the edge of a precipice, for take after take, in a temperature of sixty degrees centigrade. Poor Ludmila Tselikovskaya once spent a whole night in a coffin because Eisenstein refused to let her get out of it.

'Why did we do these things without protest? I have already suggested one reason in our deep professional respect for Eisenstein as an artist. But another cause, and of equal importance was a reflection of the war. Elsewhere in our country other people were fighting and being killed and maimed for something they believed in, and perhaps the only way we could compensate for the privilege of our own safety was to fight a battle for what we regarded as serious and lasting art. For these reasons, and despite our quarrels with him, we eventually did whatever Eisenstein asked us to.

'I have said that basically we all had a great love for him, and it may seem strange that I should admit this. For not only did he and I have so many quarrels, but he also never struck me as someone who was ever genuinely 'open' with other people unless he knew them very intimately. He was not a man to weep in the presence of anyone else, or even to confess that he might now and then be despondent or sad, and yet he had the ability to persuade all of us that we were part of the work we were doing together, and to believe in its value, and to devote all our energies to its success. One aspect of his extremely complex personality never failed to surprise me, if only because I have known so many lesser men without it, and that was his completely natural way of treating, say, a young lighting assistant as though he were as important to the production as Prokofiev. Consequently such people were transformed in his presence, and if he ever shouted at them in a fit of temper they immediately forgave him and were never angry or offended. I was often very angry myself, but they never were.

'I well remember one occasion when, in my rage, I had genuinely come to the conclusion that Eisenstein or no Eisenstein, world war or no world war, I could no longer stay in the film, that I was completely wrong for the part of Euphrosinia, and that unless I ran away from Alma Ata immediately I would wreck *Ivan the Terrible* completely and for ever. I felt like dying, quite literally. But the man who cured my depression was not Eisenstein, or at least only indirectly. It was my make-up man. "You've got no right to die," he told me, speaking very sternly indeed. "You've got to carry on with the job. There's no excuse for you to sabotage the fine thing we're all trying to make together. And now, if you'll be so kind, we'll get on with your make-up."

'That was it. Eisenstein's awareness of others was a creative one, and we all responded to it: the make-up man, the lighting assistant, the great Cherkasov, Prokofiev, myself. We were all helping to create a work of art, and we knew it. Eisenstein never compromised, and never spared himself. Nor therefore did we.'

Within a year of the first day of shooting at Alma Ata the first part of *Ivan the Terrible* was being edited, and so were sections of Part Two. On 2 February 1946 Eisenstein completed the editing of Part Two, and

Ivan the Terrible

that same evening attended a dinner-dance to celebrate the award of of the Stalin Prize for Part One. At two o'clock in the morning he collapsed on the dance floor from a heart attack and was taken by ambulance to the Kremlin Hospital. Towards the end of May he was moved to a sanatorium outside the city, and a month later was allowed to convalesce in his house in the country. He was there on 16 August to read the first published criticism of *Ivan the Terrible, Part One*, in the magazine *Sovietskoye Iskusstvo*. On 4 September the Central Committee of the Communist Party issued a statement attacking Soviet film-makers in general, and saying of Eisenstein that he 'had disclosed his ignorance of history by presenting the progressive body-guard of Ivan as being a collection of degenerates resembling the Ku Klux Klan, and turning Ivan himself, who in reality was a tough man with great strength of character, into someone as feeble and hesitant as Hamlet'. Stalin personally disliked the film, and although agreement was later reached in principle between the two men, Part Three was never continued, and Part Two was shown in public only ten years after Eisenstein's death.

It is almost as unfair to assess *Ivan the Terrible* on the basis of its two completed parts as to applaud or condemn *Bezhin Meadow* by reference to the work of restoration by Sergei Yutkevich and Naum Kleiman. Nor was it helped by the gap of fourteen years which separated the first public showings of Part One and Part Two, for, as Jay Leyda has rightly observed, there is a deliberate stylistic transition between the films which demands that in fairness to Eisenstein they must be judged together and not separately. The qualities of Part One are 'majestic' and 'ceremonial', and the increase in human passion towards the end of the film leads logically to the 'flaming bitterness and physical violence' of Part Two. Part Three would have opened out the trilogy, with more exteriors, more crowd movements, and more battle sequences, in contrast to the ominous interiors and the human tensions of Part Two. Nor was *Ivan the Terrible* helped by the drastic change in national and international moods between 1944, when Part One was first shown, and the release of Part Two in 1958. Mosfilm Studios had been evacuated at the height of the Nazi bombardment of Moscow, and the war on the Russian front increased in ferocity as Eisenstein was preparing to shoot in Alma Ata. There was a strong mood of patriotism, in the best sense of a word too often maligned, and a public appetite for those great figures of the past with whom the people could identify, who were larger and tougher than themselves and yet were also their own ancestors, their national family tree. Alexander Nevsky was such a figure, and so was Ivan the Terrible. When Part One of Eisenstein's film was first shown in the Soviet Union the war in Europe had another six fierce months to run, though it was clear by then that the land of Ivan IV would not be conquered. It is easy, in these terms, to understand why the film was so successful in its own country, and why it was awarded the Stalin Prize.

Its reception abroad was less enthusiastic, though for two of those who had met Eisenstein in the West it was one of his finest achievements. Charles Chaplin, in a personal message to Eisenstein, called it 'the greatest historical film ever made', and John Grierson summed it up in these words:

'I personally believe that Eisenstein was most glorious and most truly himself in his last film, *Ivan the Terrible*. I know that many critics have regarded it as an artificial piece of work, full of pasteboard spectacle and cardboard characters, but it always remains in my memory as something not only visually memorable but also, and above all, vastly quiet; and when a great artist – a Michelangelo, for instance – can discipline himself to be so very quiet, then he surely is a very great artist indeed.'

It was in *Ivan the Terrible* that Eisenstein filmed in colour for the only time in his life, and most effectively for a banquet sequence that was made strictly in terms of his own theories:

'The principal condition for the use of colour in a film is that it must have an essential dramatic purpose. In this respect it is exactly like music. As music in films is only admirable when it is absolutely necessary, so colour is only available when it is necessary. Colour and music are both good when, and only when, they contribute to a more complex and effective expression of what the film is trying to say. For myself I want the ideas to *explode* into colour, and in doing so to create an image that is a fundamental part of the drama itself.'

For the second half of 1946 and all of 1947 Eisenstein's health prevented him from further film-making, though he prepared notes for an epic to be made entirely in colour on the subject of Moscow's eight-hundred-year history. He wrote some new essays and edited old ones, kept in touch with his students and wrote reminiscences. He also echoed his behaviour after the condemnation of *Bezhin Meadow* by publishing a magazine article which generally accepted the criticism of Part Two of *Ivan the Terrible*. As his fiftieth birthday approached he became increasingly depressed, and much of his personal writing suggested that he was uncertain of the extent of his own achievement and the meaning of human life in general. Among those who saw him regularly at this time was Grigori Rostotsky:

'Early in 1948 Eisenstein phoned me one evening and said: "What is all this I hear about a plan to celebrate my fiftieth birthday?" I told him quite openly that there was indeed such a proposal, and moreover that it had my full support. "In that case", he said, "all is well. It so happens that they've asked me who should make a speech, and I suggested yourself." I think I replied with a poor joke, agreeing to do it if he made it worth my while. Then, very suddenly, his tone changed, losing all its gaiety and becoming almost solemn. "You know, of course, that your speech will in fact be for my funeral, not for my birthday."

'He often spoke of death at that time, and I am quite sure that he was in considerable pain, though he never referred to it, and certainly never showed it. He was usually as cheerful as ever, and often full of jokes, so that most of his friends had begun to accept those references to death as just another joke in his repertoire. "But Sergei Mikhailovich," I said, "why do you keep talking about death? You know as well as I do that we're all going to celebrate your fiftieth birthday, and it will be a wonderful occasion. So please stop making all these ghoulish references to your imminent death."

'On 23 January 1948 he celebrated his birthday. Just over a fortnight later I had to visit Leningrad on business, and Eisenstein gave me a letter to deliver to Nikolai Cherkasov, the actor who had played Ivan the Terrible, and who was a close friend of his. When I got back to the station in Moscow I thought I might phone Eisenstein from a call-box, to tell him that I had seen Cherkasov and delivered the letter. Unfortunately I hadn't the proper coin in my pocket, and so I decided to put off the call until the following day, especially as the mornings were the best time to catch him at home. But at six o'clock in the morning I myself received a phone call from his flat. The caller was his domestic help – a loyal and magnificent woman known to us all as 'Aunt Pasha' – and she told me that he had died during the night.

'For me there is a personal sequel to that story. All my life I had lived in Moscow in Chertvertov Selskokhozyastvinov Street, and one day a few years ago my wife came into my study and said: "Many congratulations!" I was surprised. As far as I was aware I had done nothing to deserve that word. Then she explained herself. "From now on you'll be living in Sergei Eisenstein Street. They're going to change the name." Which was the truth, and today the wall of our house bears the name-plate of my old teacher.'

Maxim Strauch described the last day of Eisenstein's life in these words:

'One day in February 1948 he showed me a sheet of paper on which he had been writing in red pencil. Suddenly, at a point halfway across the page, the hand-writing had broken off in a sharp plunging curve. "That", he said with a strange smile, "is the graph of my disease." During the night of that same day I had a telephone call from Eduard Tisse. He had just received a call himself from "Aunt Pasha" who always slept in a room near Eisenstein's study, and her message was that he had collapsed. Tisse and I went to the flat at once, but when we arrived it was already too late. Eisenstein was dead.'

He left a widow, his former assistant Pera Attasheva. Eisenstein, so dependent in childhood on his mother, and so shy and reserved in his adult friendships, lived his life without any deep relationship with women. Yet there were two women who worked with him closely: Pera Attasheva, whom he knew since the 1920s, and Elizabeta Sergeyevna Teleshova, who had helped him with the casting of *Bezhin Meadow* and *Alexander Nevsky*, and who died during the war. Pera Attasheva, although she lived in a different flat, had become his legal wife and was now his heiress.

His body lay 'in state' before the funeral, and among those who stood in mourning beside it were the Minister for Cinematography, Ivan Bolshakov; the film directors Grigori Alexandrov, Vsevolod Pudovkin, and Dmitri Vasiliev; the novelists Ilya Ehrenburg and Alexander Fadeyev; Eduard Tisse; the dramatist Vsevolod Vishnevsky; the theatre director Yuri Zavadsky; the painter and stage designer Pyotr Williams; the actresses Serafima Birman and Lyubov Orlova; and Sergei Prokofiev. He was buried in the Novodevichy Cemetery, not far from the graves of Chekhov, Scriabin, and Mayakovsky.

'Immortality', Eisenstein once wrote, 'is not a form of after-death collaboration between one generation and the next, but the very ideal for which each succeeding generation struggles and dies. For me immortality can only come from the constant fight for the revolutionary ideal of human freedom.'

Maxim Strauch and G. V. Alexandrov in the apartment of Eisenstein's widow, Moscow, 1969

NOTES AND REFERENCES

Unless otherwise stated the words of Eisenstein himself were selected and translated for the B B C documentary by Naum Kleiman, and the other quotations are transcripts of recordings or interviews made for the same film. The translations of the Russian statements are by Ariadne Nicolaeff.

1

1. This was the subject of Eisenstein's first published article, in the journal *Lef* in 1923. A long extract from it appears as a chapter in *The Film Sense*, translated and edited by Jay Leyda (London, Faber & Faber, 1943).

2

1. *Sight and Sound* (British Film Institute, Autumn 1956).
2. *Film Forum* (New York and London, 1946).
3. *The Film Sense*, op. cit. Translator's note.
4. Léon Moussinac, *Sergei Eisenstein: An Investigation into his Films and Philosophy* (Paris, Editions' Seghers' Cinema d'Aujourd'hui, 1964; English translation by D. Sandy Petrey, New York, Crown Publishers Inc, 1970).
5. Ibid.
6. Nikolai Lebedev, *An Outline History of Cinema in the U.S.S.R.* (Moscow, 1947). Quoted by Jay Leyda in *Kino* (London, George Allen & Unwin, 1960), p. 241.
7. In addition to the words spoken by Maxim Strauch in an interview with the author, this passage contains further details from an article by him in the journal *Yunost* (Moscow) which was later published in English in the magazine *Sputnik* (Moscow, Novosti Press Agency, 1968).

3

1. Léon Moussinac, op. cit.
2. Ibid.
3. 'Eisenstein's Lectures in London', B B C Third Programme, December 1949.
4. Ibid.

4

1. Jay Leyda, *Kino*, p. 302
2. 'How Eisenstein Worked with his Students', Bulletin of the Centre for Soviet and East European Studies (College of Communications and Fine Arts, Southern Illinois University of Carbondale, Winter 1973).
3. The Manifesto was published as a Statement in *Zhizn Iskustava* (Leningrad), and an English translation appeared in *Close Up* (London) in October 1928. Léon Moussinac (op. cit., pp. 154–6) quotes it in full.
4. A translation of Eisenstein's speech by Ivor Montagu was published in *Life and Letters Today* (London, Autumn 1935).
5. Any summary of the Conference must gratefully acknowledge its debt to the accounts in the biographies of Eisenstein by Marie Seton (London, The Bodley Head, 1952) and by Ion Barna (Bucharest, Editura Tineretului, 1966; English language edition translated by Lise Hunter and edited by Oliver Stallybrass, London, Martin Secker & Warburg, 1973). Especially valuable is Jay Leyda's excellent analysis in *Kino*, pp. 318–20.
6. Marie Seton, op. cit., pp. 260–2.
7. Longer extracts from Shumyatsky's statement are quoted in a different translation by Léon Moussinac, op. cit., pp. 157–60.
8. Eisenstein's statement first appeared in an English version in the review *International Literature No. 8* (Moscow, 1937).
9. Two notable exceptions were Ivor Montagu and his wife, who found Eisenstein to be in his customary high spirits.
10. *Kino*, p. 361.
    The word 'Terrible' is misleading, and a fairer English translation is 'Awe-inspiring'.

BIBLIOGRAPHICAL NOTE

These notes are limited to publications in English, and they exclude the enormous number of critical essays about or by Eisenstein that have appeared in magazines and anthologies. Nor do they take into account the obvious fact that virtually every history of the cinema, however objective or however personal, has always devoted several pages to his work.

The most complete biography of Eisenstein is by Marie Seton (London, The Bodley Head, 1952). Although this is an extremely personal account and parts of it are controversial, nevertheless her book remains an essential starting-point for any serious student of Eisenstein.

A more recent and less provocative biography is that of the Romanian, Ion Barna (English language version published in London by Secker & Warburg, 1973), which denies any attempt 'to analyse Eisenstein's work as an artist . . . but investigates its emotional sources, the circumstances in which it was born, the special concurrence of sensory and social events that determines the condition for the appearance of a work'. As such it is a very stimulating and generally accurate book.

Much shorter is *Sergei Eisenstein* by the late Léon Moussinac, and subtitled 'An Investigation into his Films and Philosophy' (English translation by D. Sandy Petrey, New York, Crown Publishers, 1970). Moussinac, like Marie Seton, knew his subject personally, and his book is particularly useful for its account of Eisenstein's visit to France. It also includes the Manifesto *Sound and Image* (by Eisenstein, Pudovkin, and Alexandrov), passages from Boris Shumyatsky's statement about *Bezhin Meadow* and the full text of Eisenstein's 'autocriticism', and extracts from interviews with Alexandrov, Pera Attasheva, Nikolai Cherkasov, and Maxim Strauch.

Another stimulating memoir, also by a personal friend of Eisenstein, is Ivor Montagu's *With Eisenstein in Hollywood* (Berlin, Seven Seas Publishers, 1968). Written with considerable wit and charm it not only includes a valuable section about the conference of La Sarraz but contains two of the scenarios written in Hollywood – *Sutter's Gold* and *An American Tragedy*. The fullest account of the circumstances leading to the abandoning of *Que Viva Mexico!* is to be found in *Sergei Eisenstein and Upton Sinclair: The Making and Unmaking of Que Viva Mexico!* (Bloomington, U.S.A., Indiana University Press, and London, Thames and Hudson, 1970).

Eisenstein's scenarios, in one form or another, have been published frequently in English. *Battleship Potemkin*, *October*, and *Alexander Nevsky*, edited by Jay Leyda and translated by Diana Matias, appear in a single volume (London,

Lorrimer Publishing Ltd, 1974). This valuable book also contains the extract from the projected film *1905*, which was the basis of *Battleship Potemkin*, as well as parts of a planned sequel to *October* and the final scenes of an earlier version of *Alexander Nevsky*.

The entire scripts of *Ivan the Terrible*, including Part III, edited by Ivor Montagu and translated by Ivor Montagu and Herbert Marshall, are also available (London, Secker & Warburg, 1963).

Of Eisenstein's own work in English translation, the most accessible books are: *The Film Sense*, translated and edited by Jay Leyda (London, Faber & Faber, 1943), *Film Form* and *Film Essays*, both by the same editor and translator (London, Dennis Dobson, 1951 and 1968 respectively), and *Notebooks of a Film Director*, translated by X. Danko and edited by S. Yurenev (London, Lawrence & Wishart, 1959).

Invaluable for any student of Eisenstein is *Kino*, Jay Leyda's admirable history of the Russian and Soviet cinema (London, George Allen & Unwin, 1960), which describes, fully and effectively, the social artistic context of Eisenstein's work in the U.S.S.R.

Two books shortly to be published seem certain to be of considerable importance: Herbert Marshall's *The Biography of a Film – Battleship Potemkin* (New York, Avon Books), and Eisenstein's own *Autobiography*, translated and edited by Herbert Marshall (London, Dennis Dobson).

FILMOGRAPHY

(In the case of completed films the year of first public screening is shown)

1923 Eisenstein directed a short film sequence for inclusion in his production of Alexander Ostrovsky's play *Enough Folly in a Wise Man* at the Proletkult Theatre in Moscow. It was photographed by B. Frantzisson, and those taking part in it included Grigori Alexandrov, Mikhail Gomorov, Maxim Strauch, Vera Yanukova, and Eisenstein himself.

1925 *Strike.* Script by Valeri Pletnyov, I. Kravchunovsky, Grigori Alexandrov and Sergei Eisenstein. Photographed by Eduard Tisse and Vasili Khvatov. Directed by Sergei Eisenstein, assisted by Grigori Alexandrov, I. Kravchunovsky, and A. Levshin. The actors were from the Proletkult Theatre, including Alexander Antonov, Mikhail Gomorov, Maxim Strauch, Grigori Alexandrov, and Judith Glizer.

1925 *1905.* This film, conceived to celebrate the Revolution of 1905, was abandoned when Eisenstein decided to concentrate on a single episode – the mutiny on the battleship *Potemkin*. The material shot for 1905 was never edited. The script was by Nina Agadzhanova-Shutko, and the photography was by Eduard Tisse.

1925 *Battleship Potemkin.* Script by Sergei Eisenstein from a treatment by Nina Agadzhanova-Shutko and Sergei Eisenstein. Photographed by Eduard Tisse. Directed and edited by Sergei Eisenstein. The Assistants to the Director were Grigori Alexandrov, Alexander Antonov, Mikhail Gomorov, A. Levshin, and Maxim Strauch. The titles were designed by Nikolai Aseyev. The leading players were Alexander Antonov, Vladimir Barsky, Grigori Alexandrov, A. Levshin, and Mikhail Gomorov.

1927 *The General Line.* The original title of the film that is known as *Old and New*, its production was interrupted when Eisenstein agreed to make *October*. When he returned to it he changed it almost completely. Script and direction were by Eisenstein and Alexandrov, and the photography was by Eduard Tisse.

1928 *October* (sometimes known in an English-language version as *Ten Days That Shook the World*). Written and directed by Sergei Eisenstein and Grigori Alexandrov. Photographed by Eduard Tisse, assisted by Vladimir Popov and Vladimir Nilsen. The Assistants to the Directors were Maxim Strauch, Mikail Gomorov, and Ilya Trauberg. The leading players were Nikandrov (as Lenin), N. Popov (as Kerensky), Boris Livanov (as Cabinet Minister), and Eduard Tisse (as a German). The rest of the cast was almost entirely drawn from the citizens of Leningrad.

1929 *Old and New*. Written and directed by Sergei Eisenstein and Grigori Alexandrov. Photographed by Eduard Tisse, assisted by Vladimir Popov. The Assistants to the Directors were Maxim Strauch and Mikhail Gomorov. The leading players were Marfa Lapkina (as the Peasant Woman), Vasya Buzenkov, Kostya Vasiliev, Father Matevei (as the Priest), Chukmarev (as the Kulak), Khurtin (as a Peasant), and Sukhareva (as the Witch). All of these were non-professional actors. (NB: This film, though very different from the partly completed *The General Line*, has been shown as *The General Line* in an English-language version.)

1929 *The Storming of La Sarraz*. A short satirical film made by delegates to the International Congress of Film-makers at La Sarraz in Switzerland. Shot in one day, and never cut, it has since been lost. Directed by Sergei Eisenstein, Hans Richter, and Ivor Montagu. Photographed by Eduard Tisse. The leading players were Janine Boussinouse (as the Spirit of the Artistic Film), Bela Balasz (as the Commander of the Army of the Commercial Cinema), Sergei Eisenstein (as the Commander of the Army of Independence), Léon Moussinac, Hans Richter, and Walter Ruttman.

1929 *Woman's Joy is Woman's Woe*. Produced by Lazar Wechsler. Directed and photographed by Eduard Tisse. A film on the subject of abortion, shot in Zürich and completed in Paris. Eisenstein's contribution to the film is still disputed, though it is certainly possible that he either directed or supervised the direction of one sequence. In 1935 Lazar Wechsler produced a revised version of the film, adding new sequences with synchronized sound, and this is the only version available.

1930 *Romance Sentimentale*. Directed by Sergei Eisenstein and Grigori Alexandrov. Photographed by Eduard Tisse. A short 'musical' film made in Paris, and largely the work of Alexandrov. It was the first time that Eisenstein, Alexandrov, and Tisse had worked with 'sound', and the opening sequence, directed by Eisenstein, is particularly imaginative.

1930 *(Untitled)*. In London Eisenstein appeared as a Policeman in a project that was part of a film course organized by Hans Richter. Less than a minute of the uncut rushes remain.

1930 *Sutter's Gold*. A script, based on the novel *L'Or* by Blaise Cendrars and written by Eisenstein, Alexandrov, and Ivor Montagu, was submitted to, and rejected by, Paramount.

1930   *An American Tragedy*. This version of Theodore Dreiser's novel, also by Eisenstein, Alexandrov, and Montagu, met the same fate, and at the same hands, as *Sutter's Gold*.

1931   *Que Viva Mexico!* To be produced with the financial backing of Upton Sinclair, this film was planned in six episodes, five of which were shot before the film was stopped by Sinclair. Written and directed by Sergei Eisenstein and Grigori Alexandrov, and photographed by Eduard Tisse. The unedited material remained in the U.S.A. (latterly in the Museum of Modern Art in New York) until 1974, when it was sent to Moscow. A technical and production team, including Grigori Alexandrov and Sergei Yutkevich, are assembling it.

　　　In the meantime the following films have been made from Eisenstein's footage:

　　　1933　Thunder Over Mexico. Produced by Sol Lesser.
　　　　　　Death Day. Produced by Sol Lesser.
　　　　　　Eisenstein in Mexico. Produced by Sol Lesser.
　　　1939　Time in the Sun. Produced by Marie Seton, and edited by Roger Burnford.

In addition several 'shorts' were made by the Bell and Howell Company: *Conquering Cross, Idol of Hope, Land of Freedom,* and *Spaniard and Indian.*

1932   *MMM*. A comedy, written by Eisenstein, which never got beyond the casting stage. The leading parts were to be played by Maxim Strauch and Judith Glizer.

1937   *Bezhin Meadow*. Based on the story with the same title by Turgenev.
and   Script by Alexander Rzheshevsky, with revisions by Isaac Babel and
1956   Sergei Eisenstein. Photographed by Eduard Tisse. Leading players: Vity Kartshov, Boris Zakhava, and Elena Teleshova. The film was cancelled when sixty per cent of it had been shot. The negative is assumed to have been destroyed by flooding when the Mosfilm Studios were damaged in an air-raid during the Second World War. In 1956, and using the 'frames' from the material that had been preserved, Sergei Yutkevich and Naum Kleiman constructed a montage of 'stills' from the film, based on the original scenarios, and using music chosen from the symphonies of Prokofiev.

1938   *Alexander Nevsky*. Script by Sergei Eisenstein and Pyotr Pavlenko. Directed by Sergei Eisenstein, with the collaboration of D. I. Vasiliev, Photographed by Eduard Tisse, with A. Astafiev and N. Bolshakov. Music by Sergei Prokofiev. The leading players were: Nikolai Cherkasov (as Alexander Nevsky), Nikolai Okhlopkov (as Vasili Buslai), Alexander Alrikosov (as Gavrilo Olexich), Dmitri Orlov (as Ignat), Vasili Novikov (as Parasha), and Nikolai Arsky (as Domash Tverislavich).

1939 *The Ferghana Canal.* A short documentary to celebrate the opening of the canal. Directed by Sergei Eisenstein, and photographed by Eduard Tisse.

This was made from the material shot for a proposed film about the history of Central Asia which was abandoned at the beginning of the Second World War.

1944 *Ivan the Terrible (Part I).* Written and directed by Sergei Eisenstein. Photographed by Eduard Tisse (exteriors) and Andrei Mosvin (interiors). Music by Sergei Prokofiev. Lyrics by Vladimir Lugovsky. The leading players were: Nikolai Cherkasov (as Ivan IV), Ludmila Tselikovskaya (as the Tsarina Anastasia), Serafima Birman (as Euphrosina), Pyotr Kadochnikov (as Vladimir), Mikhail Nasvanov (as Prince Andrei), and Alexander Alrikosov (as Prince Fyodor).

1958 *Ivan the Terrible (Part II).* Although completed in 1946 this film was not shown publicly until 1958.

The main credits are the same as those for *Ivan the Terrible (Part I)*.

INDEX